INSTITUTE OF PSYCHIATRY
Maudsley Monographs

MAUDSLEY MONOGRAPHS

HENRY MAUDSLEY, from whom the series of monographs take its name, was the founder of the Maudsley Hospital and the most prominent English psychiatrist of his generation. The Maudsley Hospital was united with the Bethlem Royal Hosital in 1948, and its medical school, renamed the Institute of Psychiatry at the same time, became a constituent part of the British Postgraduate Medical Federation. It is entrusted by the University of London with the duty to advance psychiatry by teaching and research.

The monograph series reports work carried out in the Institute and in the associated Hospital. Some of the monographs are directly concerned with clinical problems; others, less obviously relevant, are in scientific fields that are cultivated for the furtherance of psychiatry.

Joint Editors

Professor Gerald Russell
MD, FRCP, FRCP (Ed),
FRC Psych.

Professor Edward Marley
MA, MD, DSc., FRCP,
FRC Psych.

Assistant Editor

Dr Paul Williams
MD, MRC Psych., DPM

with the assistance of

Miss S. E. Hague, BSc. (Econ), MA

INSTITUTE OF PSYCHIATRY

Maudsley Monographs

Number Thirty

Patterns of Improvement
in
Depressed In-Patients

By

MALCOLM LADER, DSc, PhD, MD, FRCPsych, DPM

*Member of Scientific Staff, Medical Research Council
Professor of Clinical Psychopharmacology,
Institute of Psychiatry, University of London,
Honorary Consultant, Bethlem Royal and Maudsley Hospitals*

REUBEN A. LANG, BA, MSc, PhD

*Clinical Psychologist, Alberta Hospital,
Edmonton, Canada*

GLENN D. WILSON, MA, PhD, FBPS

*Senior Lecturer in Psychology,
Institute of Psychiatry, University of London*

OXFORD UNIVERSITY PRESS

1987

Oxford University Press, Walton Street, Oxford OX2 6DP
Oxford New York Toronto
Delhi Bombay Calcutta Madras Karachi
Petaling Jaya Singapore Hong Kong Tokyo
Nairobi Dar es Salaam Cape Town
Melbourne Auckland
and associated companies in
Beirut Berlin Ibadan Nicosia

Oxford is a trade mark of Oxford University Press

Published in the United States
by Oxford University Press, New York

British Library Cataloguing in Publication Data
Lader, M.H.
Patterns of improvement in depressed in-patients.—(Maudsley monographs; no. 30).
1. Depression, Mental—Treatment I. Title II. Lang, Reuben A. III. Wilson, Glenn,
1942– IV. University of London, Institute of Psychiatry V. Series
616.85'2706 RC537
ISBN 0–19–712154–3

Library of Congress Cataloging in Publication Data
Lader, Malcolm Harold.
Patterns of improvement in depressed in-patients.
(Maudsley monographs; no. 30)
Bibliography: p.
Includes indexes.
1. Depression, Mental—Chemotherapy. 2. Antidepressants. I. Lang, Reuben A. II.
Wilson, Glenn D. (Glenn Daniel) III. Title. IV Series [DNLM: 1. Antidepressive
Agents—therapeutic use. 2. Depression—drug therapy. 3. Psychopharmacology–methods.
W1 MA997 no. 30/WM 171 L153p]
RC537.L32 1987 616.85'2706 87–12202
ISBN 0–19–712154–3

Set by Spire Print Services, Salisbury
Printed in Great Britain
at the University Printing House, Oxford
by David Stanford
Printer to the University

Preface

Depression is a complex emotion and physical state which affects a substantial proportion of the population at one time or another in their lives. It ranges from a mild disturbance of mood to a major life-threatening illness. In many cases the presence of a suicidal risk influences management. In the past 30 years, the advent of electroconvulsive therapy and of the modern antidepressant drugs led to great improvements in treatment. Patients no longer languish in hospital with 'Bedlam Melancholia'. Also, interest has arisen in the relationship between the various facets of depression – the emotional, somatic, cognitive, and so on.

We took the opportunity of monitoring the response of depressed in-patients to antidepressant therapy and thereby evaluating the relationship between various aspects of depressive phenomenology. This monograph is based on a thesis presented in the University of London by Reuben Lang. The work was carried out jointly between the Department of Pharmacology (ML) and the Department of Psychology (GW). It represents a joint effort of the type becoming increasingly common in psychiatric studies where a variety of techniques is needed to attack a clinical problem.

M.L.

London   R.A.L.

March 1987   G.D.W.

Acknowledgements

We are indebted to the following consultant psychiatrists of the Bethlem Royal and Maudsley Hospital for allowing access to patients under their care: Dr J. L. T. Birley, Dr J. R. W. Christie-Brown, Professor J. C. Gunn, Dr R. Kumar, Dr A. D. Leigh, Dr P. J. Noble, Professor R. Levy, Dr M. Crowe, Professor M. Shepherd, Dr E. H. Hare, and Dr F. Post. We thank Marie Eagle for typing the numerous versions of the manuscript with such care.

This research was supported by Medical Research Council funds and by the Social Sciences and Humanities Research Council of Canada.

Finally, we are grateful to all the patients who, in the midst of their emotional turmoil, so willingly agreed to take part in the study.

Contents

Tables and figures

1. Introduction

The term 'depression' variously describes a mood, a symptom, a syndrome and a disease entity (Kline, 1969). For most people, depression is ephemeral, mild, and a response to an upsetting event. For about 3 persons in 1000, however, it is so severe as to result in a hospital admission. Of the reported range of 8 to 14 per cent of suicides in all mental disorders, depressives account for between 27 and 74 per cent (Silverman, 1968).

Depression has at least four identifiable characteristics: (1) a 'central mood'; (2) a 'cognitive distortion' factor; (3) various 'psychomotor deficits' and; (4) a host of 'somatic complaints' (Kidman, 1985). Any of these factors can be part of any psychiatric and physical disorder and, in the depressive state itself, they need not all be present to establish the primacy of that condition (Nelson & Charney, 1981). Certain other features, not necessarily associated with the core features of the phenomena of depression, contribute to a variety of forms of depression, for example, irritability, general hostility, social withdrawal, anxiety and tension, and delusional thinking.

Through the influence of both theory and clinical practice, classification of depressive disorders has also taken many forms, each based largely on rather discrepant assumptions (Kendell, 1976; Kringlen, 1985). The neurotic-psychotic distinction is mainly based on considerations of 'severity', whereas the distinction between the manic-depressive and melancholic depressive types depends on the type of episodes in the patient's history. The traditional reactive-endogenous typology reflects both historical data, for example, the presence or absence of any precipitating life stressor, and some clinical features.

The accummulated evidence on aetiology for this mode of classification is not very strong. Kendell's (1976) review suggests that the causal relationships between type 'A' (endogenous-psychotic) and type 'B' (reactive-neurotic) depressions remain largely unresolved. Moreover, to add to the confusion, the terms, neurotic-psychotic and reactive-endogenous have been used interchangeably by many authors (Eysenck, 1970; Mendels, 1970; Paykel, 1971; Roth *et al.*, 1972).

Clinical investigation of emotions, moods, and states has also been an important aspect of psychological research into depression (Bibring, 1953; Beck, 1967). Even though definitions of emotion abound (see Izard, 1971), the largely unobservable and often subtle nature of affective reactions has always created problems for psychology. Nevertheless, the importance of emotion in depressive disorders seems beyond question. Emotions are not 'epiphenomenal' and they influence physiological functioning (Lader, 1975), behaviour following emotional arousal (Seligman, 1974) and personality functioning (Foulds & Bedford, 1975).

As depression may vary from momentary and mild fluctuations of normal affective states to severe and protracted mood disorders, it would seem reasonable to evaluate mood disturbance in terms of the ongoing dynamic behaviour of the individual, rather than retrospective note-taking of previous symptoms. In severe form, most affective states (i.e., fear, anger, sadness, or irritability) are clearly seen as pathological by virtue of their intensity, pervasiveness, persistence, and interference with a person's usual social and psychological functioning. Presumably, with the trend toward the investigation of 'states', and toward more longitudinal studies of mood states, clinical workers will identify the sequence of recovery of the major mood variables.

However, apart from the large-scale P-technique factor analyses (P = person) of Raymond Cattell and his co-workers, depression has been little studied in terms of an exaggerated mood disturbance continuous with normal affect states. To date, very few studies have focused on the daily mood fluctuations or periodicity in mood of depressed patients over time (see Little & McPhail, 1973; Stallone *et al.*, 1973; Huba *et al.*, 1976).

As the literature review will show, most studies relevant to depression have the disadvantage of focusing on only one domain of human functioning and, even then, performance of clinical improvement is only examined twice, pre- and post-treatment. What happens in between is largely unknown. Moreover, the results vary considerably from in-patient to out-patient samples and are influenced by the severity of the disorder, the type of illness, treatment modality used and age. Many of these factors are frequently uncontrolled and vitiate comparisons between studies.

Whereas analogue investigations with normal subjects (including depressed college students) are of great importance in the study of depression as a normal affect state that may have continuity with various types of clinical depression, they are of limited use when evaluating the more distinct psychomotor, behaviour and illogical thinking effects: these have to be studied in psychotic and depressed patients. However, as many of the laboratory studies to be reviewed will show, many parallels exist between normal and clinical anxiety and normal and clinical depression, and these support the view that various depressive states can be arrayed along a continuum from a normal period of self-limiting low mood at one end to psychotic suicidal hopelessness at the other (Kendell, 1968; Eysenck & Eysenck, 1976; Ni Bhlorchain *et al.*, 1979).

The intention of the present study was not to resolve the classification issue. Only minimal emphasis will be placed on psychiatric nosology of depression. Instead, we concentrate on a longitudinal analysis of the clinical features of depression, with a view to generating complete recovery functions for the major variables under scrutiny. The specific aims were to study a fairly circumscribed group of hospitalized depressives in order to detect by a number of psychological tests the various shifts in thinking, memory, mood patterns, bodily symptoms and motor functioning which occur with clinical improvement. While the topic of depression has been extensively researched, it is still unclear if the emotions, behaviours, or thinking processes of the depressed person follow a predictable pattern of recovery, or if they fluctuate toward eventual improvement in some random pattern. Of great scientific interest, too, is the question of precisely what variables are important in the development (and maintenance) of the clinically depressed state over time.

A further important question concerns the 'sequencing' among moods, overt behaviours, memory, learning, and motor deficits, particularly with respect to those changes which precede the resolution of depressed mood.

The repeated measures, longitudinal research design is clearly needed to supplement much recent experimental research on depression, emphasizing the 'situation-specific' manipulation of moods, beliefs, or attitudes. In order to fill the gap left by studies using too few subjects or limited testing, the present investigation was designed to examine, in finer detail, the variability of a larger number of moods.

2. Review of the literature

MOODS AND THEIR MEASUREMENT

An important aspect of the exploration of depressive phenomena, as well as of normal functioning, is the study of an individual's moods, emotions, or feeling states (Izard, 1979; Sjöberg & Svensson, 1976). However, emotion has always created problems for the clinical investigator. Definitions of emotion abound in the literature (for example, Izard, 1971; Strongman, 1973; Plutchik & Kellerman, 1980). Basic to this problem of definition is the inherent difficulty in isolating emotional phenomena.

While some progress has been made in identifying specific patterns of physiological responses associated with different emotions (for example, Ax, 1975; Lader, 1975), very little current psychological research involves the phenomenological aspects of emotional states in depression. Yet the quality and intensity of the feelings experienced by clinically depressed subjects seem their most characteristic, unique and distinct features. To achieve a more thorough understanding of the phenomenological-experiential patterns of emotions, one must distinguish between the qualitatively different feeling-states, and evaluate the intensity of such states as they change over time.

Because of difficulties of method, transitory feeling-states were for a long time largely ignored in psychological research. Attempts to develop rating scales for the quantitative assessment of emotional states have been infrequent, as objective research methods for effectively measuring these continually changing, subjective inner experiences have not been available. Over the past two decades, however, different investigators have developed structured self-report scales that show promise as measures of transitory moods and emotional states.

Since the 1950s, transitory states, like enduring moods, have been of much interest in empirical psychological research into depression. Much of the research on measuring moods has utilized Mood Adjective Check Lists (MACLs). These lists comprise mood-describing adjectives, such as glad, sorry, elated, depressed, which are used to complete the sentence, 'I feel . . ..' Such checklists were developed in the 1950s by Nowlis (1961). Subjects are asked to rate themselves on these adjectives on a mood-intensity dimension. Although four bipolar mood dimensions were originally posited, a series of factor analytic studies produced 12 unipolar mood-factors, at least six of which have been replicated by Borgatta (1961) and McNair & Lorr (1964).

MACLs have proved convenient for measuring feelings of shorter duration, i.e., states of mind, and are used in pharmacological research to measure changes in drug-induced moods (Nowlis, 1961, 1970). Recent trends of research concern mood dimensions in personality disorders (Hoffman & Peterson, 1970), mood and self-esteem (Coleman, 1975), mood and cognitive functioning (Sjöberg & Johnson, 1976), diurnal variation in mood (Taub & Berger, 1974), and mood in relation to age, personality, time, and day (Christie & Venables, 1973). In particular, the mood of activation has been investigated by Thayer (1967, 1970, 1971), who obtained four independent unipolar factors, termed general activation, high activation, deactivation-sleep, and general deactivation.

Another, more promising, technique for measuring daily intra-subject mood variation is the Visual Mood Analogue Scale (VMAS) (Aitken, 1969; Aitken & Zealley, 1970; Luria, 1975, 1979). The value of the VMAS has gained increasing recognition since its description by Aitken in 1969 (though originally suggested by Freyd in 1923). The VMAS consists of a 100 mm line at one end of which is an adjective like 'happy' and at the other, the adjective 'sad'. The patient is required to mark the line according to his feeling at the time. The VMAS score is calculated by measuring the distance in millimetres from the left end of the line to the patient's vertical mark. Thus far, the VMAS has proved to be a reliable and valid instrument which can conveniently provide repeated assessments of a patient's mood (Little & McPhail, 1973; Folstein & Luria, 1973; Hart *et al.*, 1976; Slavney *et al.*, 1977; Luria, 1975, 1979; Hamilton, 1979).

For clinical purposes, such scales have the advantage of extreme simplicity. Ratings can be adapted to the appropriate time interval, for example, over the past week, day before, or at the present time. Such simple linear scales have proved useful in the self-evaluation of anxiety symptoms (Lader & Wing, 1966) and have been used to detect differential treatment effects (Shaw, 1977; Taylor & Marshall, 1977). Another important feature is that the obtained scores can be arcsine transformed if the data need normalizing (Aitken, 1969).

Generally, then, personality inventories measure traits, while mood scales assess feeling states. One exception, Spielberger's State Trait Anxiety Questionnaire (STAI), provides a self-report measure of both. However, as emotional states fluctuate often quite unpredictably over time, repeated 'state sampling' is the preferred way to chart the cyclic pattern of depressed mood during treatment.

Notwithstanding, self-report measures like the VMAS can be criticized on many grounds. The items are ambiguous and convey discrepant meanings to different people; many people are reluctant to admit their faults; people are simply too unaware of themselves to respond honestly. Still, even adults or adolescents with at least dull–normal intelligence (i.e., WAIS IQ range: 85–100) can describe how they feel at a particular time.

Most people are willing to reveal how they feel during a therapy hour, or while performing an experimental task, or how some drug is affecting them, provided they are asked specifically about their feelings, and the feelings were experienced recently. Moreover, the VMAS is such a simple self-report scale that even very ill and uncooperative patients can complete the slips daily with only a few exceptions (Luria, 1979). Of course, the clinician or experimenter who uses the VMAS to measure rage, ecstasy, or other emotional states must motivate his patients or subjects to provide accurate data about themselves. Even so, the 24-hour reliability of the VMAS (Luria, 1979), diurnal sensitivity (Aitken, 1969), or hourly validity in mood-altering drug studies (Hart *et al.*, 1976) is sufficiently high to confirm its clinical usefulness.

While reliability coefficients from a test-immediate retest analysis of mood ratings are high (around 0.90), McNair & Lorr (1964) found test-retest reliabilities to be somewhat lower for 150 neurotics who rated themselves before and after four weeks of treatment (in the region of 0.61 to 0.69). This is presumably due not to any loss of internal consistency or stability of the rating scale, but to genuine intraindividual mood fluctuation over time. As MACL or visual analogue scales are *state* as opposed to *trait* measures of emotionality, 'the researcher would expect and indeed hope for low test-retest reliability' (MacKay, 1980, p. 514).

Of the handful of factor analytic studies performed on visual analogue scales, a factorization of 16 VAS by Bond & Lader (1974) produced only three factors, which were labelled 'Alertness',

'Calmness' and 'Contentedness': two showed clear drug effects (i.e., the residual effects of butobarbitone sodium and flurazepam). Herbert, Jones & Dore (1976) factored a total of 732 protocols obtained from 38 subjects over a 5–22 day period in a study of mood before and after a night's sleep (factoring the occasions as subjects). Two factors emerged, one relating to psychomotor performance, the other to nuances of affect. Using 19 bipolar scales, Meddis (1969) also extracted three factors from the mood self-ratings of 70 subjects. Thus, most of the variation for the 16–19 item VAS scales factored in these three studies can be accounted for by two or probably three stable factors. While these studies are important, all the subjects were normal volunteers, and so the factor structure for an equivalent or larger number of VAS scales with a clinically depressed population might be usefully established.

MOOD DISTURBANCE IN DEPRESSION

Over the last half-century, the empirical literature on the psychology of depressive states and conditions has burgeoned. Depression, either in its clinical forms (not necessarily pathological) or as a transient mood disturbance, represents an especially challenging and intriguing topic. Yet depression, originally thought to be the most clearly conceptualized field of study, has in many ways proved indefinable.

Depression has been used to describe momentary and mild variations of normal and necessary affect states (Bibring, 1953) as well as severe and protracted clinical disorders (Mendels, 1970). It has been used to describe a relatively enduring, pessimistic cognitive style (Beck, 1974, 1976), or a character style (Blatt, 1966) in which 'there is an unusual susceptibility to dysphoric feelings, a vulnerability to feelings of loss and disappointment, intense need for contact and support, and a proclivity to assume blame and responsibility and to feel guilty, (Blatt, 1974, p. 109).

As a clinical disorder, depression has been used to describe the severe reactions of young infants separated from their mothers (Spitz, 1954), feelings of abandonment and an urgent sense of needfulness (Freud, 1917/1957; Bowlby, 1980), as well as intense and severe standards with a pervasive sense of failure, transgression, and guilt (Mosher, 1979). Dependency in depression has been interpreted as a seeking of love and approval to offset feelings of guilt and unworthiness or, alternatively, as a function of feeling weak, helpless, and needing support and protection (Seligman, 1974; Beck, 1967; Schmale & Engel, 1975). Other mood-states, such as anger or hostility, are commonly found in depression and decrease with clinical improvement (Mayo, 1967; Friedman, 1970); measures of hostility do not, however, differentiate between depressed and non-depressed states (Pilowsky & Spence, 1975; Perris *et al.*, 1979).

Also, many cases have a constant fear of losing a dear one (Rochlin, 1965). often with markedly ambivalent feelings about one's self and others. This 'sense of loss' (real, symbolic, or fantasized) has been put forward as a necessary condition for most depressive illnesses (White, Davis & Cantrell, 1977). Extending this view, Brown & Harris (1978) have offered some new evidence to suggest that past loss by *death* (of a family member, relative, or close friend) is a characteristic precipitant of psychotic depression; whereas past loss by *separation* is more likely to relate to the neurotic/hostile type of depression.

Despite the wealth of available descriptive phenomenology, more exacting models (or concepts) to account for the role of moods in maintaining or diminishing the depressive syndrome have lagged behind. Part of this muddle is, perhaps, due to the 'mixed bag' that the term 'depression' denotes; the concept is used interchangeably to describe a mood, a symptom, a syndrome, and a discrete diagnostic entity.

But as a mood, depression is ubiquitous. Furthermore, under the rubric of depression is included almost every symptom in psychiatry (Schwab *et al.*, 1965; Watts, 1966). Until recently, however, there has been a broad consensus that depression is primarily an affective disorder (Robins & Guze, 1972; Perris, 1973; Akiskal & McKinney, 1975; Klerman, 1977; Spitzer, Endicott, Woodruff & Andreason, 1977).

While the unmistakable meaning of 'affective' is that an alteration in mood is the primary symptom, expressions of depressed mood may be found in any type of clinical depression, including grief and situational reactions as well as the other major psychotic syndromes, such as schizophrenia. Yet, such unambiguous complaints as helplessness, hopelessness, or despair are recognizable in most instances, and should be adequate markers of depression. In any case, when the 'depressed mood' alone is the screening criterion, an undetermined proportion of depressions may escape recognition.

Theoretically, feeling worthless or guilty may reflect the original cognitive distortion of depression, i.e., a faulty self-perception (Beck, 1963) or a facet of the neurotic-like, poor self-concept, causing the individual to perceive himself as inadequate, sinful or guilty.

Implicit in this and other formulations is the issue of whether depression can be viewed as a single, unitary disorder or as several phenomena that need separation conceptually. Is it, for example, basically a mood disorder (Spitzer *et al.*, 1977; Hamilton, 1974) or potentially a thought disorder (Beck, 1976; Kovacs & Beck, 1978)? While the evidence for each is fairly extensive, the general view supports Beck's premise of the dominance of cognition over mood (Beck, 1974, 1976; Mahoney, 1974). While psychoanalytic theory also holds that bodily symptoms are secondary to affective change, Beck contends that all manner of symptoms, whether somatic, motivational, or affective, are secondary to the primary cognitive defect.

How to evaluate 'depression' has always been a problem (Ciccetti & Prusoff, 1983) as the term has come to encompass a broad range of entities, clearly heterogeneous despite some similarities (MacFadyen, 1975). Most clinical and research observations and theoretical formulations have considered depression primarily as a clinical disorder, focusing on negative affect, lethargy, fatigue, and somatic-vegetative disturbances, including complaints of sleep loss, poor appetite, digestive problems and loss of sexual interest. To date, depression has been little investigated as a variable affect state that may relate over time with other aspects of learning, memory, or perceptual-motor functioning which are usually impaired during the depressive episode.

Learning and memory, for example, are disrupted during both manic and depressed phases to an extent that often reflects the intensity of the mood disturbance (Henry, Weingartner & Murphy, 1973). Clinical experience shows that many patients who complain of depressed mood regularly experience poor memory, a lack of ability to concentrate, and a tendency to more passive behaviour. To date, few studies analysed mood or feeling states over time, or their covariance in response to tricyclic medication or psychotherapy. Nor has the history of treatment of depressive disorders attempted any systematic synthesis of thinking about affects, feelings, and emotions.

Reviewing the recent evidence, the wide variation in the

theoretical formulations of human depression is not surprising: depression represents a complex of aetiology, symptoms, and treatment response. Perhaps the difficulty has been in trying to subsume the phenomenology of mood within conceptually simple, even naive research orientations such as bipolarity, activation, the trait-state dichotomy, the factorization of mood protocols, and so forth.

Again, longitudinal studies of how specific feeling states covary over time have been sparse (Cattell *et al.*, 1972; Stallone *et al.*, 1973; Huba *et al.*, 1976; Teasdale, Fogarty & Williams, 1980). It is important to detect any time lag between different mood variables, and to determine whether there are other variables independent of mood change which remain unaltered by a given strategy.

Mood variability, too, has always posed a problem for researchers, often giving an unrealistic picture of the true level of severity (Beck, 1967; Zuckerman, 1976). Mendels (1970) proposed that moods are not variable at different severity levels, but this is largely unsupported by more recent findings (Little & McPhail, 1973; Slavney *et al.*, 1977), and from general clinical observations of varying mood in mild-to-severely ill neurotic and psychotic depressives.

That a host of bodily symptoms accompany dysphoric mood is well known (Schwab *et al.*, 1965; Mowbray, 1972b; Hamilton, 1976). Such somatic complaints, including sleep disturbances, generally precede the reduction of depressed mood (Vaisanen *et al.*, 1978; Beck *et al.*, 1979).

Mood profile patterns of depressed individuals are complex. Anxiety and depressive feelings are common to all types, though affective expression may be somewhat muted in the retarded type of depression. The milder forms of depression comprise perhaps 75 per cent of the people diagnosed as depressed by clinicians (Beck, 1976). Cognition and mood are closely related, perhaps even inseparable. Because the depressive spectrum does include moods, feelings, and affects as major components (Schuyler, 1974), a finer analysis of the pattern of change for various mood variables as the depression lifts should yield useful data on the psychological recovery process.

SYMPTOMS OF DEPRESSION

Defining criteria

The clinical features of depression not only vary enormously between patients and fluctuate in intensity from day to day or diurnally
but also respond differentially to treatment. Although the bound-
aries between mood, symptom, and syndrome are sometimes
unclear, this section will focus on the somatic symptoms of primary
and secondary affective disorders (Katz, 1971; Weissman, Prusoff
& Pincus, 1975).

In 1966, Munro introduced the concept of 'primary' affective
disorder into psychiatric nomenclature. He defined it as an affective
disorder 'with no history of a psychiatric disorder apart from
affective disorder or (depressive or cyclothymic) personality'. However, one immediate ambiguity is that while there may be no
pre-existing psychiatric disorder, the possibility of a serious medical
illness is not considered.

More recently, Robins and co-workers (1972) have debated the
practicality of the primary-secondary scheme, as opposed to the
reactive-endogenous dichotomy, and note that it avoids the problem
of identifying aetiological factors. Nor does it depend on the often
confusing patterns of current symptom severity. Another related
problem is that the pre-existing symptoms may suggest a psychiatric
disorder but fall short of the formal criteria for an illness. And,
lastly, the time of onset of an affective disorder relative to a
non-affective illness is often indeterminable.

The affective disorders involve a disordered emotional state as a
fundamental element. In this grouping are the anxiety neuroses,
depressive illnesses, and manic conditions. Defining criteria used by
three researchers to classify depressive persons are listed in Table 1.

A close relationship also obtains between depressed mood and
the severity of bodily symptoms. Because of the dichotomous form
of many depression-rating scales (i.e., the MMPI 'D' Scale, Pilowsky
Inventory), the yes–no format actually provides little or no
discrimination for the degree of intensity or frequency of any
symptom, as the total score relates mainly to quantity (Ilfeld, 1976).
Note, too, that in assessing somatic symptoms of the depressive
state, the intention is not to measure 'mental illness', nor is it
implied that the presence of bodily symptoms is in some way

equivalent to, or prognostic of, a diagnosable mental illness (Sells, 1968; Eysenck & Eysenck, 1976).

One of the first problems that researchers into clinical depression must consider is the multidimensional nature of the depressive condition itself. Not only are there symptoms which are mutually exclusive, for example, loss of appetite and binge eating, as Depue & Monroe (1978) point out, but some facets of depression occur in predictable patterns to lend partial support to the notion of discrete psychiatric entities. As depression can include almost any symptom known to psychiatry (Mowbray, 1972a), only the more definitive features linked to the depressive experience can be listed (Table 1).

Though the prevalence of bodily symptoms has been well established in previous work, the time dimension and sequencing of somatic discomfort have been little explored. Until recently, psychologists have neglected the study of the *rates* of response and *pattern* of symptom reduction in clinical depression. Much of the pharmacological research on depression, reviewed by Morris & Beck (1974), suggests that approximately 60 to 70 percent of depressed people improve significantly within a 4–6 week period. Considering this, it would seem important to elucidate the approximate duration of the physical complaints of depressives, though preferably not retrospectively.

One of the earliest reviews of manifest symptoms in diagnosable depressive episodes is that of Lewis (1934, 1938). Described in fine detail from a careful analysis of 61 cases are such characteristic signs and symptoms of depression as tiredness, loss of weight, headaches, 'aches and pains', stupor, palpitations, retardation, slowness of gait, indigestion, constipation, abdominal discomfort, nausea, constriction of the larynx, and so forth. While depressed mood is justifiably viewed as the central feature of the depressive state, Lewis (1934) observes that '. . . the infrequency of complaints about bodily ills (at least in his sample) would suggest that this is not a considerable factor in determining which symptoms he reports'. Among other factors, the patient's preoccupation, his self-abasement, the stress that symptoms cause him, and his attitude toward his illness also figure prominently in the patient's own subjective experience in the clinical interview.

In the same review, Lewis (1934, p. 351) points out that '. . . it may be said in general that variations from day to day, or within a few days are common, . . . the sequence of clinical states, however, is anything but uniform, and the same may be said of the duration of

Table 1. *Different criteria needed for the diagnosis of depressive disorder*

Somatic[1]	Equal somatic and psychological[2]	Somatic and psychological[3]
Both needed	*Both needed*	*One needed*
Dysphoric mood	Dysphoric mood	Dysphoric mood
Definite onset	Definite onset	No definite onset
Plus	*Plus*	
5 of below = probable diagnosis	4 of below = probable diagnosis	
6 of below = definite diagnosis	5 of below = definite diagnosis	
Anorexia	Anorexia or weight loss	Poor appetite
Weight loss		Weight loss
Insomnia	Insomnia	Early morning awakening
Feelings of fatigue	Feelings of fatigue	
Decreased sex interest	Loss of interest in job, social activity or sex	Loss of interest in social activity or sex
Constipation		
Slow thinking	Slow thinking or poor concentration	Lack of reactivity
Poor concentration	Guilt feelings	Inappropriate guilt
Suicidal ideas	Suicidal ideas or wish to be dead	Suicidal behaviour or wish to be dead
Agitation	Agitation or retardation	Agitation or retardation

[1] Essentially identical to criteria of Cassidy *et al.* (1957).
[2] Identical to criteria of Feighner *et al.* (1972) except that Feighner requires a specific duration of affective symptoms.
[3] Adapted from Mendels and Cochrane (1968).

the various phases'. This daily variation received much attention among early British and German psychiatrists as there accrued evidence of periodicity. Kraepelin could demonstrate that melancholics, as compared with healthy people, display in the afternoon a greater ability to calculate, an increase in muscular strength, and a tendency to perform better at selective tests. For many patients, depression and retardation are more conspicuous in the morning; during the course of the day, depression and retardation lessen, even in severe cases. According to Lewis, 'the slow and painful waking-up of patients reaches a point, as the day goes on, where they can be got to occupy themselves a little and can more easily be got to talk and even laugh' (Lewis, 1934, p. 350).

PSYCHOMOTOR PERFORMANCE IN DEPRESSIVE DISORDERS

Psychomotor retardation is a major symptom complex manifested as delayed or slowed spontaneous and evoked purposeful motor activity, and is a consistent feature of depression (Miller, 1975; Kendell, 1976; Nelson & Charney, 1980). Clinically, the lowered psychomotor pace of the depressive has been variously described as lowered response initiation (Beck, 1967), slowness of movement (King, 1975, Greden & Carroll, 1981), rigidity of the musculature (Depue & Monroe, 1978), slowed reaction time (Court, 1964), and retarded speech (Lewis, 1934, Fleiss, Gurland & Cooper, 1971).

Psychomotor performance deficits

The psychomotor inhibition so characteristic of the clinically depressed patient can take on many forms. Depth of depression, an important factor, has in some studies been shown to be fairly independent of impaired psychomotor functioning (Friedman, 1964); Granick, 1963) but clearly related to the severity of the depressive reaction in others (Shapiro & Nelson, 1955; Payne & Hewlett, 1960). Almost without exception, normal subjects are fastest on psychomotor speed tests, followed by neurotics, depressives, acute and chronic schizophrenics, with brain-damaged subjects the slowest (Miller, 1975).

By far the largest category of performance measures, the *psychomotor* tests, are inexpensive, easy to administer and score, seldom time-consuming, and fairly sensitive to antidepressant drug effects or the presence of neurological deficits. As the earlier studies of Fleishman (1960) and Uhr (1960) have indicated, specific components exist. Control precision, for example, involves fine, highly controlled muscular movement, and one measure of this factor is the Pursuit Rotor Test. Another factor, response orientation, is concerned with the skill needed to make the appropriate movement in response to a stimulus, for example, simple or choice reaction time tasks. However, a global measure of, say, pursuit rotor tracking gives no direct information on the optimal learning period, the patient's control or hand movements, or whether some degree of 'automatization' (performing a skill without conscious attention as in touch typing) had occurred (Frith & Lang, 1979; Lang & Frith, 1981). Overall, psychomotor movements are fairly independent of one another; factor analysis has failed to identify any general 'movement factor' (Fleishman, 1960; King, 1961).

Over the last 35–40 years, a vast literature has compared normal subjects and various psychiatric subtypes on many psychomotor responses (reviewed by Fleishman, 1960; King, 1965, 1975; Miller, 1975). The regular appearance of motor dysfunction among depressive patients is well-established (Shapiro & Nelson, 1955; Payne & Hewlett, 1960; Beck, 1967; Hamilton, 1974).

One of the earliest studies (Franz & Hamilton, 1905), reports that most depressive patients who engaged in a daily routine of physical exercise significantly increased their psychomotor tempo. In his classic observational study of depressives, Lewis (1934) draws attention to the lowered psychomotor speed, and the improvements or deteriorations in this factor over the course of treatment. Marked diurnal variations in motor behaviour were noted, not only in the endogenously/psychotically depressed patients but also in the reactive types.

Psychotic depressives usually present with an obvious marked psychomotor deficit. Typically, the abnormality is slowing of psychomotor response together with a large intrasubject variability (Friedman, 1964; King, 1965). For psychotically ill patients, the estimated severity of depression is highly correlated with the patients' degree of psychomotor slowing (Shapiro, Nelson & Maxwell, 1960; Shapiro & Nelson, 1955; King, 1965). The severity issue is obscured by problems of patient heterogeneity, unspecified selection criteria, and the patient's level of psychophysiological arousal during testing.

As the severity of the behavioural disorder reflects the degree of psychomotor slowness across different patient groups, changes in the clinical condition of a given patient may correlate with the speed of simple motor performance (Hall & Stride, 1954; King, 1965; Beck, 1967; Cecchini *et al.*, 1978; Tsutsui *et al.*, 1979). For example, depressive patients who respond favourably to electroshock therapy improve significantly in simple psychomotor speed (Fisher, 1949; Heshe, Roder & Theilgaard, 1978).

PSYCHOLOGICAL PERFORMANCE TASKS

Simple motor performance tests

Reaction time is a pure factor (Fleishman, 1960) with motor and sensory components and can be measured to visual (Zubin, 1975) or auditory stimuli (Bond & Lader, 1975; Friedman, 1964). As a measure of response latency, reaction time provides a useful index of the level of vigilance of the subject. Both simple (i.e., discriminability of one stimulus) and choice reaction time (i.e., requiring the subject to switch his attention from one stimulus to another, as well as from one response to another), already in use in Wundt's laboratory before 1900, were adopted to assess attention in depressive and schizophrenic disorders (Woodworth & Schlosberg, 1961).

During the 1950s other evidence began to emerge to suggest that a normal-neurotic-depressed-manic/schizophrenic continuum might exist with respect to psychomotor performance, with considerable within-group variability. Acute schizophrenics and manic-depressives had much slower reaction times than neurotic patients (Huston & Senf, 1952), the early schizophrenics resembling the manic-depressive patients (Hall & Stride, 1954). Additionally, Hall and Stride (1954) note that reaction time is dependent on age.

Recently Cornell, Suarez and Berent (1984) studied simple reaction time (SRT) and motor reaction time (MRT) in three groups: melancholic depression ($N = 14$), less severe depression ($N = 14$) and 14 normal control subjects. Although the three groups did not differ on the SRT measure, the less severe patients differed significantly from controls on the MRT measure but did not differ from melancholics. Evidence from other studies (Bruder, Yozawitz, Berenhaus & Sutton, 1980; Byrne, 1976; Martin & Rees, 1966) also suggests that depressed patients exhibit a generalized deficit in motor activity involving a wide range of tasks and behaviours.

At least two studies, with contradictory results, should be briefly mentioned. On a series of trials using choice RT, Pascall and Svensen (1952) found no differences on the first trial between groups of psychotics, neurotics, and normals. Over successive trials, though, the normals improved most. Using an unpleasant noise to motivate subjects reversed the deficits (by a raised level of psychophysiological arousal), so that the patients' performance resembled that of the normal subjects.

Colbert and Harrow (1968) compared depressives and controls on the Bender-Gestalt reaction time task. No significant differences were recorded perhaps because only 20 per cent of the depressives were objectively retarded on test performance, while the majority showed only the universal subjective retardation common to clinically depressed subjects.

Reaction time simple or choice, has however, been shown to improve with change in clinical status (Hall & Stride, 1954) and can also be speeded up to some extent by special incentives, stimulant drugs, or a heightened state of psychophysiological arousal. Longer hospitalization periods may increase reaction time (Resnick, 1965).

Tapping rate

Tapping rate is a pure measurement of wrist-finger speed (Reitan, 1955) which, despite its simplicity, is considered one of the most sensitive components of psychomotor ability. Tapping speed is slower than normal in psychotic, manic-depressive, or schizophrenic disorders (Shakow & Huston, 1936; Shapiro, Nelson & Maxwell, 1960). With well-matched control groups of normal and depressed patients under identical task demands, the distinction becomes more blurred (Friedman, 1964). Performance levels of brain-damaged or severely disturbed patients fall well below those of normal and neurotic subjects but neurotic and reactive depressives, in turn, perform much like normals (Shapiro & Nelson, 1955). However, female patients diagnosed as depressed in two parallel studies (Weckowicz *et al.*, 1972, 1978) had a slower tapping rate than non-depressed controls (hospital in-patients).

Gibson Spiral Maze

This test of psychomotor speed and accuracy, introduced by Gibson (1965), has proved to be a useful and convenient measure of eye-hand co-ordination. The test consists of a spiral pathway bestrewn with small printed circles which serve as obstacles to be avoided. Using this measure with depressive patients, Mayo (1966) found it sensitive to the characteristic speed loss that accompanies dysphoric mood, and observed that performance improved with clinical recovery over a six-week trial.

Blackburn (1975) evaluated 106 patients on the Gibson Spiral Maze. There were 18 in each of six groups – ill and recovered unipolar and bipolar depressives and bipolar manics under two conditions, distraction (external and internal) and no distraction. Without distraction, no differences in age, sex, or intelligence were noted before or after recovery for any of the three types of patients. Bipolar depressed patients were significantly slower than unipolar or manic patients, who did not differ.

Digit Symbol Substitution Test (DSST)

This particular test, involving a combination of coding ability and associative mental functioning, is a widely used subtest of the Wechsler Adult Intelligence Scale (Wechsler, 1958). The task on this timed test is to match certain pairs of numbers and figures by referring to a charted code.

As depressives recover with electroshock therapy digit-symbol scores improve (Fisher, 1949; Callagan, 1952). Beck, Feshbach & Legg (1962), controlling for age and level of vocabulary, found digit-symbol performance to be independent of Beck Depression Inventory (BDI) scores and clinical diagnosis. Scores on the digit-symbol test did relate, however, to the severity of reported depression. Neurotic depressives did not differ from nondepressed patients; neither did psychotic depressives from schizophrenics.

Within diagnostic categories, the more severely ill the patient, the lower the digit-symbol score. The fact that psychotic depressives code fewer items than neurotic depressives who differ little from non-depressed, pathological groups (except for schizophrenics) suggests that degree of motor slowing and severity of psychopathology are positively related. Psychomotor deficit may not be solely an index of depression, as it is also common to schizophrenic, brain-damaged and mentally handicapped persons.

Depressed female patients tested by Weckowicz and colleagues (1972) scored lower than elderly control subjects. Even after matching for verbal ability, no interaction effects for depression with age were observed. Luria (1974) also concluded that digit-symbol scores varied inversely with the degree of dysphoric mood, but only for 'clearcut cases of psychotic depression'. No such relationship emerged for Luria's neurotic depressive or non-affective psychotic patients. Possible sources of this unexpected result such as age, sex, or treatment effects were not examined further.

COGNITIVE DEFICITS IN DEPRESSION

Memory and concentration

Cognitive disturbances are pivotal in descriptions of depression (for example, Beck, 1967; 1974; Friedman & Katz, 1974). Although memory processes are central to cognitive functioning, only a handful of investigators have applied theories of memory (cf. Tulving & Donaldson, 1972) in an attempt to identify which aspects of memory are most affected by depression and most responsive to treatment. Depressed persons seem impaired in their retention of verbal material over short periods (i.e., 1 to 20 minutes), as well as in their later recall of the information (Cronholm & Ottosson, 1961; Payne, 1973; Prigatano, 1978).

Many depressed patients complain of 'poor memory' (Weckowicz, 1973; Beck, 1974). Some writers have reported from their clinical impressions that the patient's subjective complaints of memory disturbances are an expression of a lowered self-esteem due to depressive affect (Anthony & Benedek, 1975; White, Davis & Cantrell, 1977). In Friedman's (1964) comparison of normal and depressive subjects, short-term memory for the psychotic group was found to be 'somewhat impaired' (p. 240). Symptom severity did not significantly correlate with the poorer memory functioning of the psychotic patient.

In Cronholm and Ottosson's (1961) investigation, three operationally defined indices of memory, immediate and delayed reproduction and forgetting, were sampled by means of a word-pair test, a figure test and a personal-data test in 45 endogenously depressed patients, twenty of whom were matched with mentally healthy controls. The 20 depressed patients had impaired learning relative to the controls but did not differ in retention. Learning was not adversely affected by ECT for 42 of 45 depressed patients but retention was impaired. As Cronholm and Ottosson (1961) sum up, 'the depressive state mainly impairs learning and ECT mainly retention' (p. 199) The memory deficit is one principally of 'registration' (short-term memory) rather than of 'retention' (long-term memory), the latter being uninfluenced by clinical improvement (Cronholm & Ottosson, 1961, 1963).

In his sample of 68 elderly depressives, Post (1966) found that 11 scored in the demented range on a simple learning task, with remitted patients showing some rather modest gains. Memory deficits were related to defects in the short-term storage of new and unfamiliar material. In another study (Glass *et al*., 1981), a group of 32 moderately depressed out-patients had impaired performance on a short-term item-recognition memory task without impairment of speed or attention on two simpler tasks.

Thirty men in prison suffering from an affective disorder were divided into three groups – those with a history of manic-depressive illness, a group of unipolar, psychotically depressed men, and a group with reactive depression (Robertson & Taylor, 1985). Compared with a group of 41 prisoners who were well, all three groups showed specific impairments in dealing with spatial/holistic cognitive tasks.

Young endogenous depressives showed improved STM, with little change in retention (LTM), after a 26-day course of imipramine or amitriptyline (Sternberg & Jarvik, 1976). For the 20 of 26 patients who improved, the better the clinical remission, the greater the improvement in STM scores. Again, much as Cronholm and Ottosson (1961) found, endogenous depression is clearly related to an impairment of STM, but without any change in retention (Sternberg & Jarvik, 1976, p. 223).

Increases in intra-individual variability with age pose another series of problems in the psychometric evaluation of memory functions involving the depressed elderly (Salzman & Shader, 1979). Older depressed subjects showed impaired performance on a serial learning task (Whitehead, 1974). The Whitehead study included 24 depressives, all over 60 years of age: 12 subjects were examined before they received treatment, the remainder on remission of their depressive episode.

. Lloyd and Lishman (1975) showed that in 36 hospitalized depressives at initial testing, the higher the Beck Depression Inventory score, the more patients tend to recall unpleasant (U) experiences over pleasant (P) experiences. On retesting, from two to six months later, the Beck depression score and U/P ratio were still correlated. However, the decrease in depression scores over time was not matched by a proportional increase in the U/P ratio, though the overall trend was in the right direction. Though inconclusive, the results suggest that the readiness of recall of an experience and hedonic tone (whether pleasant or unpleasant) relate to some extent to severity of depression. Similar data were obtained by Breslow and his colleagues (1981).

Teasdale and Fogarty (1979), testing normals with a slightly modified Velten (1968) procedure, found a similar pattern for self-induced, happy or sad mood induction. Using a set of 30 cards with self-referential statements which subjects read for each mood induction, happy or sad, on two occasions, latency of retrieval for pleasant memories after depressed mood induction was significantly longer,relative to memory of unpleasant experiences. The U/P ratio was significantly smaller for the depressed as compared to happy mood induction. Neither mood induction produced disparate effect on the latency of retrieval of pleasant or unpleasant memories, nor were the U/P ratios and scores from the Beck Depression Inventory correlated, as previously noted by Lloyd and Lishman (1975).

Depressed patients also complain of difficulties in concentration. In one study, a group of fairly severely depressed patients underwent a structured interview and reported a high rate of concentration lapses, especially when reading or watching television (Watts & Sharrock, 1985). Correlations were found between such 'mind-wandering' and severity of both depression and anxiety. Abstract reasoning is also affected (Silberman, Weingartner & Post, 1983).

Depression and learned helplessness

Like Beck's cognitive model, Seligman's theory of 'learned helplessness' (Seligman, 1974, 1975; Seligman, Klein & Miller, 1976; Maier & Seligman, 1976; Abramson, Seligman & Teasdale, 1978) emphasizes the role of subjective expectations as a probable but not essential condition for depression. What is learned is 'the expectation that responding and an outcome are independent' (Seligman, 1975, p. 48).

Seligman's hypothesis, based on work with laboratory animals and subsequently with human subjects (Miller & Seligman, 1973; Hiroto & Seligman, 1975; Seligman, 1975; Seligman *et al.*, 1976), posits that reactive depression, in particular, mirrors a state of learned helplessness, characterized by the *perception of non-control*. Confirmation of this view requires that subjects exposed to the helplessness-induction procedure develop some clinical feature of depression, such as sad affect, passivity, or lowered self-esteem.

Much of the data reviewed by Blaney (1977) does not provide unequivocal support for a helplessness model of depression, since in some studies only normals (not depressives) served as subjects, the helplessness effect did not emerge at all in one study (Klein *et al.*,

1976), or only for non-depressed subjects (Miller & Seligman, 1975). After a 'helplessness session', Klein and Seligman (1976) obtained the expected shift in self-reported affect for depressed but not non-depressed subjects.

According to the reformulated hypothesis by Abramson, Seligman and Teasdale (1978), which incorporates responses to the various criticisms (Blaney, 1977; Depue & Monroe, 1978), the kind of attributions a person makes about the cause of an uncontrollable event will determine his expectation of controlling future events. In turn, this expectation determines the generality, chronicity, and type of deficits which will accompany the perception of uncontrollability.

An important issue is which type of depression (i.e., endogenous–reactive, unipolar–bipolar, neurotic–psychotic or primary vs. secondary) the learned helplessness model best relates to, if any. While it would seem more compatible with the aetiology of reactive depression, the type of deficits (namely, passivity and retarded motor activity) predicted by Seligman's model are usually absent in this depressive subtype. Seligman himself (1975) maintains that learned helplessness is a model solely of reactive depression.

Another question of interest, addressed by Seligman (1978), Depue and Monroe (1978) and Costello (1978), is the validity of analogue research with depressed students and normal controls. If the experimenter-induced depressions differ only quantitatively from more severe depressive disorders (as Abramson, Seligman & Teasdale, 1978, pp. 67–68; Seligman, 1978 contend), then the evidence in favour of a *depressive attributional style*, common to all naturally occurring depressions, must be taken seriously.

More recently, Raps, Reinhard and Seligman (1980) tested the 'learned helplessness' hypothesis with three groups of in-patients: 16 non-depressives (ND), 16 depressives (D) and 16 non-depressives (LH) given a helplessness pre-exposure. After random selection, each group was exposed to either Velten's elation therapy or mood-neutral procedure. Inescapable noise produced more depressed mood than no noise condition. Elation therapy produced larger change scores than the neutral condition for the LH group. Failures on an anagram-solving task were highest for the D neutral and LH neutral conditions, confirming that cognitive deficits result from either a helplessness induction in the LH patients or from exposure to neutral 'therapy' in depressed patients. In the elation training groups, the LH patients did best followed by the D patients.

Thus, depressives show a lower mood and smaller change scores after elation training than do non-depressed helpless, subjects.

This study, the first with psychiatric in-patients, fulfils some of the requirements of Seligman's model, since at least transient cognitive and emotional deficits were produced by a helplessness procedure. These deficits were subsequently reversible. The duration of the effects induced remains unknown as there was no follow-up. Also, while the shifts from unhappy to happy mood may not closely parallel changes in depression itself, they confirm that self-rated helplessness and sad affect are intimately related.

The role of cognition and emotion in depression

Beck's theory proposes that the core of depressive phenomena contains dysfunctional beliefs which directly influence how people feel (Beck, 1967). Thinking determines what people do. Depressive cognitive styles, according to Beck, reflect a person's 'negative cognitive triad', a demeaning view of oneself, the world, and the future.

A person's depression-inducing views are idiosyncratic, highly variable, and probably acquired early in development. As they become increasingly maladaptive, that is, associated with negative value judgements, they become 'automatic' and seriously interfere with normal functioning. Ultimately, it is the patient's 'personal paradigm' which is responsible for depression.

The notion of the primacy of cognition over affect runs counter to the traditional view of mania and depression as primarily affective disorders in which cognitive factors are secondary or peripheral. Systematic errors of thinking are often based on multiple appraisals and reappraisals of one's ability to perform adequately or be perceived positively in some social situation. These errors are not only biased but also increase the degree of depressed mood or anxiety in that person. A perceived threat of some kind may stem from the faulty conceptualization itself.

The theory holds that dysphoric mood is associated with faulty thinking but is simply a secondary effect of the depression-inducing schema (the chain of cognitions, assumptions, and premisses that guide the patient's characteristic way of responding). Specific cognitive content is thus 'chained' to a particular affect (Beck, 1971, 1974; Beck, Laude & Bohnert, 1974). Thinking pre-empts feeling.

This runs counter to the view of Lewinsohn (1974), that the

cognitive aspects of depression are 'secondary elaborations of the feeling of dysphoria' (p. 169). The low rate of response-contingent positive reinforcement, not the perception of non-contingency, is the key factor underlying depressive illness.

The relationship between hopelessness, depression, and suicidal intent has been examined in a series of studies. For example, in a group of 120 hospital referred parasuicides, both severity of depression and degree of hopelessness correlated with degree of suicidal intent (Dyer & Kreitman, 1984). However, the relationship between depression and suicidal intent was dependent on that between hopelessness and intent.

Both Beck and Seligman models assume that cognitions *cause* affect, despite the limited experimental evidence that this is so. It is equally probable that depression-related cognitions are the consequence of depression (Lewinsohn, 1974; Lewinsohn *et al.*, 1981; Zajonc, 1980; Rachman, 1981), that the direction of causation is bidirectional, that is to say, there may be a reciprocal relationship between cognition and emotion which could form the basis of a vicious cycle which would maintain the state of depression.

Two penetrating reviews have appeared recently. Bebbington (1985) describes various theories of cognitive functioning in depression and analyses them critically. He concludes that we still lack an adequate cognitive account of depression. Willner (1984) also compares various theories and also finds drawbacks to them. He finds little evidence that depressions arise out of pre-existing depressive attitudes.

Until fairly recently, evidence of Beck's cognitive model has been largely anecdotal (Beck, 1967, 1970, 1971) or correlational (Beck, 1974, 1976). Indeed, problems have been encountered in measuring aspects of cognitive functioning and styles in depressed patients (Carver, Ganellen, & Behar-Mitrani, 1985). Mood-induction procedures have also been criticized (Riskind & Rholes, 1985).

Beck's cognitive therapy (1976) aims to modify both cognitive structures and the associated automatic thoughts of unipolar depressives. Treatment is structured and directive with the use of verbal and behavioural techniques, such as activity logs, list-keeping, planning activities, scheduling pleasant events, imagery exercises, and self-monitoring of automatic cognitions (Mackay, 1982). The therapist corrects the patient's systematic errors in reasoning and instructs him how to change the way he acts on information. The person is helped to identify instances of distorted social or self-perceptions, expectancies, or faulty premises and then shown how to reverse them. If the patient is successful, distorted thinking patterns are transformed and the irrational belief in the patient's automatic thought cycle is attenuated.

In the summary of cognitive-behavioural studies of depression discussed by Beck, Rush, Shaw & Emery (1979, pp. 386–393), only two of eight studies (cf. Morris, 1975; Schmickley, 1976) used depressed clinic patients. The generalizability of data from student populations, even though depressed, to the psychopathology of depression is debatable, especially as the efficacy of cognitive treatment has been demonstrated only for unipolar, non-psychotic depressed in-patients. However, Beck (1974) earlier claims to have successfully treated 'bipolar' and 'endogenously depressed' patients with cognitive therapy.

Comparisons have been made between the efficacies of cognitive therapy and pharmacotherapy. In one, cognitive therapy proved distinctly superior to imipramine both in terms of immediate outcome and at one-year follow up (Kovacs *et al.*, 1981). Hopelessness was particularly helped by the cognitive therapy (Rush *et al.*, 1982). In another study, both forms of therapy proved equally efficacious and no additional benefits occurred from combining them (Murphy *et al.*, 1984). This finding was present in another evaluation but only with respect to patients in general practice; hospital out-patients did better on the combination than cognitive therapy alone (Blackburn & Bishop, 1983).

The role of anxiety in depression

Anxiety is an unpleasant emotional state (Lader, 1975; Klerman, 1977) which is transitory and varies in intensity over time (Spielberger, 1972). The emotional reaction to the anxiety-provoking stimulus is qualitatively unique for each individual. Even with similar emotional content, responses vary in degree as a function of differences in anxiety thresholds. Like other emotions, anxiety is not easy to assess but is integral to many psychiatric states, particularly depressive illness.

Anxiety states feature prominently in many physical illnesses and usually appear in a wide range of psychiatric syndromes. The anxiety may be chronic and sustained but more frequently is episodic, as in panic attacks. Some somatic aspects of anxiety states are epigastric discomfort, palpitations, chest pains, breathlessness, headache, paraesthesia, trembling, fatigue, sweating, flushes, dry mouth, and urinary frequency (Marks & Lader, 1973). Many biological features are altered in anxiety (Judd, Burrows & Norman, 1985).

Freud regarded anxiety as the pivotal point of all neurotic symptoms and, for many neo-Freudians today, anxiety remains the focal emotion out of which depression may emerge. Marks and Lader (1973) have emphasized that anxiety beginning after the age of 40 is usually part of a depressive syndrome. Many depressive reactions are often preceded by prodromal periods of chronic anxiety.

While most clinicians agree that many depressives have signs of uncertainty, vague and specific fears, or tension (Mendels, 1970), the various rating scales disagree as to whether anxiety should be included in measures of depression. For example, the Zung Self-Rating Depression Scale and Beck Depression Inventory contain no items to assess anxiety. Yet the Hamilton Rating Scale for Depression contains items relating to both somatic and psychic anxiety. Several investigators have argued against 'mixed anxiety and depression', emphasizing the distinction between true depression and neurotic states with prominent anxiety (Downing & Rickels, 1974; Akiskal *et al.*, 1978). Although anxiety neurosis and depressive neurosis are claimed to constitute distinct entities (Roth *et al.*, 1972; Roth, 1976), the diagnostic reliability for these two categories is fairly low (Spitzer & Fleiss, 1974). Often a mixed clinical picture is seen that complicates diagnosis and treatment (Morrison & Flanagan, 1978; Coryell, Lowry & Wasek, 1980). Some patients may be described as depressives with episodic anxiety, whereas others show continuous anxiety with some evidence of sad mood which fluctuates in intensity (Walker, 1959). Prusoff and Klerman (1974) carried out a discriminant function analysis to distinguish two large groups of all-female, anxiety and neurotic depressives only to find a difference in level of depression, not of anxiety. Of 728 cases, 35 to 40 per cent were misclassified. The relationship between depression and panic disorders is particularly controversial (Shader, Goodman & Gever, 1982; Leckmann *et al.*, 1983).

Distinguishing anxiety from depression, therefore, remains difficult not only because of the substantial overlap between the two, but because clinical therapists and theorists disagree on the most effective criteria (Mullaney, 1984). Any differences might be due not only to the predominance of one form of symptom, but also to differences in symptom intensities (Klerman, 1977).

SEVERITY LEVELS OF DEPRESSIVE ILLNESS

The practical issue of 'level of severity' is an important factor whenever normal or neurotic individuals are compared with manic, endogenous, or psychotic depressives. Severity of illness, qualitative or quantitative, cuts across all facets of depression: disturbed mood, motor retardation, illogical thinking, lack of personal motivation, or somatic dysfunctioning.

Miller (1975, p. 249) contends that retarded movement reflects the severity of illness, since performance deficits are not unique to depression nor do the diagnostic subtypes differ in this respect. Some studies of retarded motor activity indicate that disruption of motor behaviour can be quite severe (Beck *et al.*, 1962; Shapiro *et al.*, 1960; Payne & Hewlett, 1960). For example, Beck and co-workers (1962) found that digit symbol performance correlated with level of severity. Yet other investigators (Shapiro *et al.*, 1958; Weckowicz *et al.*, 1972) report that depth of depression bears no relation to performance deficits.

In their evaluation of depression, many investigators continue to rely on quantitative scores provided by the yes–no format of specific rating scales (i.e. the MMPI 'D' scale or Pilowsky Inventory) which provide little discrimination of the severity of a symptom (Ilfeld, 1976). Rating scales, continuous or categorical, should cover an adequate range of illness (Snaith *et al.*, 1971). Additional measures of the 'frequency' and 'duration' of symptoms may be helpful too. If the range of intensity is too restricted, subtle changes during the process of recovery will be missed.

Another issue relates to self-perception of depression. Paykel and co-workers (1973b) and Donovan & O'Leary (1976) have shown that the depression-prone individual is likely to over-estimate the severity of his condition. In Paykel's study, psychotic depressives underestimated the severity of their affective illness as compared with psychiatrists' and nurses' ratings; neurotic depressives showed the opposite. Thus, self-rated severity may reflect a 'selective perception' factor, with cognitive distortions in patients of their true state. Evidence for alcoholic depressives (O'Leary *et al.*, 1976) suggests that the magnitude of the subjective distortion is positively related to the severity of the depression. However, Paykel and his co-workers (1973b) were unclear as to who was the more accurate rater – psychiatrist or patient. Also, depressed persons under-estimate their performance level relative to their actual performance on timed tests (Granick, 1963; Colbert & Harrow, 1968).

Level of severity is an important predictor of psychiatric outcome (Paykel *et al.*, 1973a): the greater the pre-treatment morbidity, the more the improvement. In the Paykel study, psychotic depressives (the most severely ill) improved most, with anxious depressives showing less improvement. However, patients were not all at the same initial level of pathology on all indices. Such differences are often neglected when only *post hoc* multiple 't' tests are performed on the data.

Sex differences may relate to reports of severity. Female depressives were more likely than males to present themselves as more neurotic, to declare more symptoms, and to acknowledge more psychopathology (Shackleton, 1974).

The Zung Self-Rating Depression Scale (SDS) scores were compared in 160 men and 160 women (Blumenthal, 1975): 12 per cent of men and 32 per cent of women scored in the high range. After factoring SDS protocols for 55 male and 80 female in-patient depressives, Byrne, Boyle, & Pritchard (1977) found the two sexes to differ quantitatively and qualitatively in their ratings. The higher scores of the females were thought to reflect sex differences in subjective appraisal and perception of the questionnaire items rather than 'true' differences in the severity of the depressive state. Possible sex differences were controlled for in the scoring procedure of self-rating scales (Hamilton, 1960, 1967).

Personality attributes of depressive patients vary according to subtypes of depressive illness. Thus, non-endogenous patients are aggressive and endogenous disorder patients have high drive towards success and achievement (Matussek & Feil, 1983).

CHANGES WITH TREATMENT

Considerations of space preclude any detailed discussion of the efficacy of various antidepressant therapies but a few salient points need emphasis. Although it is generally held as an article of faith that antidepressant drugs have real efficacy, one large-scale trial showed that efficacy, although statistically significant, was very limited clinically (Johnstone *et al.*, 1980). In this unusual study, 240 neurotic out-patients were treated for 4 weeks with either amitriptyline, diazepam, amitriptyline plus diazepam, or placebo. The outcome tended to be good irrespective of medication, the only statistically significant differences from placebo being amitriptyline-related improvements in both depression and anxiety. However, inspection of the graphs in the report suggest only a modest clinical effect: for example, Hamilton Depression Scores dropped over four weeks from a mean of 33 to one of 14 in patients on amitriptyline and from 32 to 17 in placebo patients.

Six-month follow-up evaluations suggested that patients with schizoaffective disorders do worse than those with psychotic depression, with non-psychotic depressives having the best outcome (Coryell *et al.*, 1984). However, comparisons with patients treated more than 40 years ago did not reveal any improvement in long-term outcome.

The importance of adequate dosage of antidepressants has been stressed (Quitkin, 1985). Up to 300 mg of imipramine or equivalent may be needed. Unfortunately, such high doses of tricyclic antidepressants lead to major compliance problems, especially in general practice (Johnson, 1981). In more severely depressed patients, symptomatic complaints apparently attributable to unwanted drug effects are more likely to reflect the depression itself (Nelson, Jatlow & Quinlan, 1984a).

Another variable which has been evaluated is the duration of treatment. Generally speaking, 4-week trials, as in the Johnstone and colleagues' (1980) study outlined above, are less successful in discriminating between active drug and placebo than are 6-week trials (Quitkin *et al.*, 1984a). Nevertheless, because depression is a self-limiting condition, longer trials may lose drug-placebo differences as time goes on, especially in mildly ill patients.

Patients with recurrent affective disorders may, however, need prolonged treatment with at least 4–5 months symptom-free before the drug is discontinued (Prien & Kupfer, 1986). The risks of relapse and chronicity are substantial (Keller *et al.*, 1986).

Quitkin's group at Columbia University have addressed themselves to the problem of distinguishing drug-related responses from placebo responses (Quitkin *et al.*, 1984b). Weekly ratings on the Clinical Global Impression Scale were available from 93 depressed patients treated with a variety of antidepressants and 92 placebo-treated patients. Of these, 44 placebo- and 30 drug-treated patients failed to respond. Of the remaining 48 placebo-treated patients, 7 showed delayed-onset persistent patterns, 5 early-onset persistent patterns, and the remainder, 36, non-persistent patterns of improvement. Drug-treated patients comprised 26 delayed-onset persistent patterns, and 5 early-onset persistent and 32 non-persistent improvement. Thus, there was some evidence that drug response is more likely than placebo response to be delayed to 3 weeks or more and be persistent.

An extended Hamilton Depression Scale was used by Nelson and co-workers (1984a) to ascertain which depressive symptoms were the best measures of response to desipramine. Correlations with desipramine plasma concentrations were used to identify treatment-responsive symptoms. Ten were found to be associated with significant improvement and were in order of sensitivity: worthlessness, decreased appetite, depressed mood, inability to experience pleasure, decreased interest in work and activities, hopelessness, guilt, somatic anxiety, decreased energy, and early morning awakening.

One interesting study, that of Vaisanen and co-workers (1978), investigated 95 in- and out-patients in a double-blind, independent groups trial comparing the effects of 3 × 25 mg/daily dosages of maprotiline and doxepin over four weeks. Nine target symptoms were assessed at weekly intervals by a physician using a visual analogue scale (Zealley & Aitken, 1969). By the end of the third week, initial scores had decreased to about a third of their pre-treatment values. Hypochondriacal complaints and loss of weight, initially reported as slight, all but disappeared by the fourth week of treatment under both drugs. Complaints of fatigue and sleep disturbances decreased significantly from a moderate to a very slight level, both drugs having similar effects.

The doctors' overall assessment, based on a visual analogue scale (VAS), showed that both psychotic and neurotic depressives react similarly to equal dosages of maprotiline and doxepin. By the fourth week, depressive affect had been reduced to about 30 per cent on the maprotiline group and 35 per cent in the doxepin group. Interestingly, although patients were rated as having minimal signs of bodily tension by the end of treatment, psychic anxiety only shifted slightly through weeks 2 to 4. In this connection, Hamilton (1976, p. 177) emphasized that '. . . Many patients who never lose all of their symptoms do not come down to a low score on the rating scale because they still retain many of their anxieties, even though they have lost most of their depressive symptoms'.

To compare flupenthixol and amitriptyline, two groups of depressed out-patients were evaluated for six weeks under a double-blind procedure (Young, Hughes & Lader, 1976). Nearly all variables improved significantly over time. The overall severity score rated by an independent assessor declined steadily after one, three and six weeks of treatment. For the Hamilton and Beck inventories, amitriptyline and flupenthixol were equally effective in treating depression. While insomnia decreased steadily under both drugs, flupenthixol lessened anxiety and tremor scores more than amitriptyline. As before, the mean anxiety level post treatment remained higher for amitriptyline and flupenthixol than did the final assessment scores for insomnia, tremor and somatic features. Even though the trial intervals were generally two to three weeks apart, the differential rates of improvement for the various clinical measures were clearly shown.

Takahashi and co-workers (1979) conducted a double-blind study of amoxapine and imipramine with 122 depressive in- and outpatients over a five-week period. Doctor-rated symptoms improved linearly for depressive feelings, sleep disturbances, and somatic discomfort with both drugs. Anxiety and tension lessened much more slowly, as did suicidal ideation, the desire for isolation, and thoughts of persecution. The last three have a strong cognitive component. Clinical ratings were made on a five-point intensity scale by a team of twelve doctors familiar with the WHO-SADD scale. The most significant shift occurred for the severity of illness scores between weeks 1 and 2, with no change at weeks 0, 2, 3, 4, or 5. Amoxapine with a rapid onset of action and minimal side-effects was superior to imipramine with respect to somatic complaints, pain, sleep disturbances, anxiety, and tension but most significantly for psychomotor retardation. This study underscores the need to evaluate each symptom and sign of depression separately in order to capture the true variation, which is rarely uniform between the many facets of depression.

Imipramine at two dosages (150 mg and 300 mg/daily) was administered to fifty-one hospitalized depressives divided by a battery of questionnaires into types, endogenous and neurotic (Simpson, Lee, Cuculic, & Kellner, 1976). Clear differences between the dosages emerged for such factors as 'cannot sleep at night', 'tense and restless', 'felt tired' and 'losing weight'. By the fourth week, the physician's ratings on the Hamilton Rating Scale for Depression (HRSD) indicated virtually no sign of gastro-intestinal disturbances for either patient group given the higher dosage level. On the Physician's Rating Form for Depressed Patients (a nine-point scale), the 300 mg dosage had a greater overall effect than the

150 mg dosage on the number of somatic complaints and sleep disturbance in the neurotic but not the endogenous depressives. Again, over the trial period of four weeks, weight loss stopped completely for the neurotic depressives at both the 150 mg and 300 mg doses, remaining only very slightly progressive for the endogenous group. Approximately the same pattern emerged for genito-urinary symptoms, so that the neurotic depressives reported fully restored sexual functioning. Somatic anxiety in the neurotic depressives was significantly altered at both dosage levels, but changed very little for the endogenous patients. For psychic anxiety, post treatment scores stayed high for the endogenous depressives in both the 150 and 300 mg dosage groups. Similarly, scores for 16 neurotic depressives showed that patients tended to retain their anxieties. The only item of the Zung Self-Rating Depression Scale pertaining to a tense or restless feeling (item 13) remained at a moderately distressing level for both patient types, despite a significant dosage effect. The failure to respond more may be due to the brevity of the trial or to the refractoriness of the cognitive component of signal anxiety to tricyclic drugs. Evidently, the somatic features in depressive states recover faster than do the accompanying symptoms of anxiety.

Despite some disparate findings, sleep disturbances such as increased time to fall asleep, frequent awakening, and, in some cases, an increase in total time spent in bed, tend to respond early in many depressives to antidepressant drugs (Vaisanen *et al.*, 1978; Young *et al.*, 1976; Takahashi *et al.*, 1979; Amin, 1976). The extent to which sleep disturbances covary with mood-states or depressive cognitions as the depressive condition ameliorates is still largely unknown.

Rapp (1978) treated two groups of depressed out-patients with amitriptyline and amitriptyline-N-oxide for up to twelve weeks using Cronholm & Ottosson's Depression Scale (1960) comprising eight symptoms rated on a four-point severity scale. For insomnia, the most noticeable change occurred between the initial rating and that at week 1; from then to week 2 only a small improvement occurred. Most of the improvement in psychomotor retardation occurred between weeks 2 and 4, subsequent improvement being nugatory. Much the same pattern emerged for anxiety. However, in the amitriptyline-N-oxide group, the overall anxiety score was the same between the baseline and first week.

As some of the studies already reviewed present evidence of

periodicity for the symptoms of depression, it is important to see whether the various measures of depression follow different time courses. Is there indeed a time lag for certain features of depression like anxiety or devalued self-worth and not for others such as psychomotor tempo or suicidal thinking? Thus far, evidence is sparse about which, if any, of the various features of depression are functionally independent (Weissman & Paykel, 1974; MacKay, 1980). Murphy and co-workers (1974) report that more than half of the depressed patients under study recovered in 2 months or less, with great variability of recurrence rates and duration of depressive episode.

The importance of investigating symptom remission, not with a test-retest design but in terms of a treatment-dependent recovery curve over time, is emphasized by two relevant studies. The first is a retrospective analysis of 70 endogenous depressives (Kolakowska, 1975) and the second comprises a prospective examination of the course of bipolar affective disorder in the manic phase (Loudon, Blackburn, & Ashworth, 1977).

Based on reconstructed case material, symptom ratings and follow-up interviews, Kolakowska (1975) examined an all-female sample treated by tricyclic drugs. On some 25 symptoms frequently observed at the index admission, 44 of 70 patients remitted completely, becoming asymptomatic, while 26 depressives did not. These 'residual' features of the patients who remained symptomatic were emotional lability, hypochondriacal reaction, obsessionality, histrionic behaviour, and anxiety. That such enduring features of depression tend to occur with diminished social functioning has been confirmed in other research (Paykel & Weissman, 1973; Dorzab, Baker, Winokur, & Cadoret, 1971).

Assessment of change

Many depression-rating scales, doctors' ratings, and patients' self-reports have been used to assess depressed patients' clinical symptoms in response to treatment (Mowbray, 1972b; Becker, 1974; Miller, 1975; Hamilton, 1976; Beck, 1974, 1976; Raskin & Crook, 1976). Over the last decade, quantification of the depressive state has depended more on the development of depression-rating scales than biochemical tests (Hamilton, 1976) notably by Beck and co-workers (1961), Zung (1965), Hamilton (1976) and Pilowsky & Spalding (1972).

Seitz (1970) has shown that a number of self-report scales (including the Zung scale and the MMPI Depression scale) are all highly interrelated and appear to measure the same dimension, but are unrelated to ratings of depression made by experienced psychiatrists. In order to obtain a more complete picture of depressive symptoms, doctors' ratings have sometimes been combined with nurses' ratings (Raskin & Crook, 1976) or with patients' self-assessment (Paykel *et al.*, 1973b; Snaith *et al.*, 1971; Arfwidsson *et al.*, 1974). Though the concordance between self- and observer-rating scales is often quite high, they seem to measure somewhat different aspects of depressive illness (Prusoff Klerman & Paykel, 1972).

The controversy over who is the best rater of depressive symptoms – doctor, nurse, or patient – is by no means resolved. The evidence implies that doctor–nurse ratings, based on daily contacts and ward observations of the patient, are the more accurate indicator of manifest symptoms. Patients' self-ratings are ostensibly the more reliable source for gauging the type and degree of disturbed mood states experienced during the depressive episode. Of course, certain patients may be too distressed at the time of testing, or be unable to rate themselves because of loss of insight in severe psychotic depression. In fact, the patient may also be unable to distinguish between treatment side-effects and physical symptoms (D'Elia & Raotma, 1978). Perceptual distortions of symptoms in clinically depressive states also influence the patient's appraisal of his state (Beck, 1976; O'Leary *et al.*, 1976).

Predictors of outcome

Various factors have been evaluated as predictors of outcome. In one study in which 122 patients received antidepressant medication, the Newcastle Scale which classifies patients on an endogenous-nonendogenous dimension was administered (Abou-Saleh & Coppen, 1983). Patients with Newcastle scores in the middle range showed significantly higher percentage improvement than both those with low (neurotic) and high (most endogenous) scores.

In non-endogenous depressives in another study, favourable outcome was associated with greater initial severity, the break-up of an intimate relationship, and the presence of weight loss (Parker, Tennant, & Blignault, 1985). An Australian study in 12 Sydney general practices produced several baseline predictors of better outcome including a history of episodic or recurrent episodes, more severe depression, lower social class, break-up of an intimate relationship, and family support (Parker, Holmes & Manicavasagar, 1986).

Severity was also a predictive factor in the study of Stewart and his colleagues (1983). In a desipramine-placebo comparison, patients with Hamilton Depression Ratings above the median showed a significant drug effect, those below the median showed no such response. Stressful environmental events were not predictive of response to pharmacological treatments, in another study (Garvey, Schaffer & Tuason, 1984).

Patients with an abnormal personality comprised 34 per cent of a sample of depressed patients, obsessionality being the most frequent deviation (Shawcross & Tyrer, 1985). Patients who failed to respond to antidepressant treatment were more likely to have an abnormal personality than were the responders.

The prognosis of depression in old age is typically worse than that for younger patients (Murphy, 1983). Those with delusional illnesses did worse as did those with long-lived illnesses.

Other claimed predictors include the dexamethasone suppression test (Peselow *et al.*, 1985; Braddock, 1986; Gitlin & Gerner, 1986). Very variable results have been obtained. Biochemical measures lie outside the scope of this review (Healy *et al.*, 1985; Moller *et al.*, 1985, 1986). Finally, monitoring of tricyclic antidepressant plasma concentrations has received much study without firmly establishing its usefulness as a correlate of response rather than in avoiding toxicity and improving compliance (Preskorn, 1986).

3. Methods

Since many of the studies reviewed used only two time-points for clinical assessment, they could not generate a detailed recovery function nor specify when in the clinical course the various symptoms of depression remit. The intent of our study was to examine the *sequential rates of recovery* for a range of mood, symptom, psychomotor, and cognitive performance measures. It proved impracticable to include physiological indices of emotional reactivity, despite their desirability. Tests were selected for inclusion either because of their proved sensitivity to the 'signs and symptoms' of the depressed patient or because they were specifically devised to test particular functions believed to be impaired. Linear analogue scales were considered appropriate for measuring fluctuating feeling states, and a wide spectrum of scales involving different emotions was selected. Psychomotor skill tasks, self- and observer-ratings of gross somatic symptoms and indices of cognitive functioning, such as immediate memory, concentration, and paired-associate learning, were also used. Since depressed individuals are often anxious and poorly motivated we preferred brief performance tests that were easy to understand and which avoided prior learning. These tests were applied to a group of recently admitted patients diagnosed as suffering primarily from depression and undergoing treatment.

The general aim was to quantify the differential rates of recovery of the different aspects of depression. The following questions were of most interest to us:

1. Which moods, physical symptoms, perceptual-motor and cognitive deficits remit early, late or not at all during the recovery process?
2. Which pattern of recovery emerges for which moods?
3. To what extent do disturbed mood, somatic discomfort, and slowed psychomotor functioning correlate with severity of depression?
4. Is emotion mediated by thinking processes so that enhanced

self-worth and restored optimism antedate lifting of depression?

5. Are there specific features which distinguish patients with a good and poor short-term prognosis?
6. Is prognosis related to severity?
7. What is the duration of a typical depressive episode?
8. Does the degree of variability of mood alter self-rated improvement?
9. Does anxiety persist despite amelioration of depression?
10. Is memory recall or paired-associate learning less variable than mood measures?

EXPERIMENTAL DESIGN

A multiple baseline, repeated measures experimental design was used. After the patients' admission to hospital, measures were taken for the 30 to 90 days patients spent in hospital. To facilitate using powerful statistics in a repeated measures design (Marascuilo & Serlin, 1977), all variables were scaled to an ordinal level.

Demographic and life history information was obtained from the 70 patients during the preliminary screening interview. After establishing baseline values, mood-state was measured every second day, psychomotor and cognitive functions assessed at weekly intervals, and bodily symptoms reported by the patient once a week until he left hospital. Ratings on the Hamilton Scale for Depression (HRSD) were completed by a psychologist, medical registrar or psychiatric nurse at pre-treatment, and at the end of weeks one, two, three, four, five, six and in a few instances, up to nine weeks of in-patient care.

CLINICAL AND DIAGNOSTIC CRITERIA

First, each of the psychiatric consultants responsible for admissions to the in-patient wards of the Bethlem Royal and Maudsley Joint Hospital was approached for blanket permission to use his patients: none refused. The medical registrar and senior ward sister were consulted before an particular patient was approached for possible inclusion in the study.

During the initial intake interview, strict diagnostic criteria were applied to include only those patients the primary feature of whose psychiatric disorder was an abnormal, persistent mood with feelings of sadness, depression or a tendency to cry, sometimes accompanied by guilt, hopelessness, suicidal thinking or a depressed appearance.

Most patients were diagnosed by at least two psychiatrists as suffering from depression of the reactive (neurotic) or endogenous (psychotic) type. At least five out of ten diagnostic criteria had to be met (Feighner *et al*., 1972): (1) dysphoric mood with or without an external reason; (2) psychomotor retardation; (3) weight loss; (4) insomnia or early awakening; (5) lack of reactivity; (6) loss of interest in work, sex or social activity; (7) slowed thinking; (8) suicidal wishes/ideas; (9) inappropriate guilt; and (10) previous episodes of similar psychopathology with full recovery in between.

The criteria of Spitzer, Endicott and Robins (1978) were then applied, so that all patients admitted to the study were suffering from an unequivocal depressive disorder. The quantitative inclusion criterion was a rating over 26 on the Hamilton Rating Scale for Depression (HRSD). Further *Entry criteria* were that patients: (a) be aged between 20 and 60 years; (b) be not pregnant; (c) clinically depressed for at least one month; (d) be admitted to the studies not earlier than 3 months after any electroconvulsive therapy (ECT); (e) be functionally debilitated because of depression (for example, away from work, socially isolated, having suicidal thoughts, unable to cope and so forth) and, (f) should not be treated by their family practitioner or any other doctor or hospital following admission. *Exclusion criteria* were any history of organic disease of the brain, epileptic disorders, serious abuse of alcohol or drugs, evidence of myocardial, renal or hepatic diseases, schizophrenia, or a personality disorder.

Thus, patients were included if they were depressed qualitatively (Feighner *et al*., 1972; Spitzer *et al*., 1978) and quantitatively (total HRSD scale score ≥ 26), were medically healthy, and suffered from neither schizophrenia nor a personality disorder.

INFORMATION TO PATIENTS

The subjects were told that the study was being conducted to learn more about the experience of people who enter hospital with a major complaint of depression or suicidal intent. It was explained that depressed people may experience changes in their normal functioning. Some changes may be quite obvious; others may be more subtle. Patients were then told that we were asking their co-operation in finding out why they came into hospital, and in detailing the aspects of depression experienced at the moment, and over the time spent in hospital. We recognized that patients might not experience all these features during their hospital stay, but we were interested to know how a person's thoughts, moods, behaviours and physical discomfort that may accompany the experience of depression itself change during treatment. We explained how the regular evaluations involve completing some self-rating scales of feelings, together with some simple psychological tests. The patient was then asked if the aims and course of the study were clearly understood, and any questions that arose were answered. If, after this careful verbal explanation, the patient was fully agreeable, then formal written consent was obtained from him.

TESTING PROCEDURES

1. Observer ratings

After consent was obtained, information on demographic, medical and family history was obtained, first by a medical registrar and, separately, by a clinical psychologist during a formal interview on the hospital ward. Details provided by the patient were noted on the Intake Information Form adapted from Sudilovsky and co-workers (1975, p. 57). The questions covered four content dimensions: Demographic Data (for example, age, sex, education, occupation); Present Illness (for example, precipitating factors, symptoms, severity and duration); Past Medical History (for example, previous treatment, number of admissions, age of onset); and Family History (mental illness in first-generation probands only). Thus, we obtained personal details relating to present functional capacity, duration of the current episode, previous treatment, type of symptom, age of onset, social class, and incidence of psychopathology in first-generation family members. This information, together with the medical history, was later analysed to relate demographic and social history factors to symptom remission, severity of illness and final outcome.

Next, each patient was rated on the Hamilton Rating Scale for Depression (HRSD) by the attendant medical registrar to establish a baseline. Ratings of 19 items were based on an hour's interview with the patient and information extracted from the nursing and psychiatric notes. The symptoms rated were as follows: (1) Depressed mood; (2) Suicide; (3) Guilt; (4) Initial insomnia; (5) Middle insomnia; (6) Delayed insomnia; (7) Work and interests; (8) Retardation; (9) Agitation; (10) Psychic anxiety; (11) Somatic anxiety; (12) Gastro-intestinal symptoms; (13) General somatic symptoms; (14) Hypochondriasis; (15) Loss of insight; (16) Genital symptoms; (17) Depersonalization; (18) Paranoid symptoms; (10) Obsessional symptoms. The intensity of each symptom was evaluated every week on a 3 or 5 point scale from 0 (no symptoms) to 2 or 4 (extremely severe). (See also Figure 1, p. 53). The day the first therapeutic response was recognized was also carefully recorded. A 7-point global rating of severity of illness was made at weekly intervals.

2. Performance tasks

Psychomotor tasks were considered particularly important in measuring the effects of depression on motor reactivity. Several tasks were chosen involving different psychomotor skills, sometimes combined with perceptual and cognitive components. The subject came the day after interview to a quiet sideroom and was seated at a desk. Testing started after a few minutes' conversation and took between 30 and 45 minutes.

(a) Tapping rate

The patient was first shown how to tap the key using the index and middle fingers. He then practised for 5 seconds with his preferred hand. Tapping instructions were modified from those of Reitan (1955), in that the patient was given only one 30-second trial. The patient was asked to tap as quickly as possible. The key was connected to a portable Sanyo calculator, with a resettable electronic counter which recorded the number of key depressions during the 30-second trial. Patients were tested weekly until discharge.

(b) Symbol Copying Test (SCT)

The symbols used were the same as those for the DSST (see below), but the subject only copied them. Ten equivalent versions were available to minimize practice effects. To begin, the examiner completed the first three symbols of the sample as a demonstration. The patient then filled in the next seven blank spaces. Subjects were told to copy the symbols in order, not to erase, and not to skip any. It was also stressed that perfect reproduction was not essential. The patient then copied symbols for 90 seconds. The time in seconds per item was calculated. The symbol copying task was administered weekly.

(c) Digit Symbol Substitution Test (DSST)

Next, the DSST was given. Ten equivalent versions were available. The subject was instructed to match certain pairs of numbers and figures by referring to the charted code at the top of the sheet. Each page had a code table, with the numerals 1 to 9 in the upper box and a series of nine symbols arranged in the lower squares. There were four rows of 25 double boxes, ten of which were used to demonstrate the task. As with the SCT, the examiner filled in the first three blanks and the patient the next seven. A 90-second trial was allowed and the time per item calculated. Testing took place weekly.

(d) Gibson Spiral Maze

The maze (Gibson, 1965) is a design printed on a card of about 25×30 cm. The design is spiral in form and presents a circular pathway 235 cm in length bordered by heavy black lines. The spiral begins at a centre point and curves outwardly, with printed circles in big type which dot the whole length of the pathway. The subject had to trace his way with a pencil out of the centre of the spiral without touching any of the smaller $\frac{1}{4}$-inch diameter circles along the pathway which serve as obstacles to be avoided. Two scores were obtained: the number of obstacles or walls of the pathway touched by the pencil and time taken.

3. Cognitive tasks

(a) Logical memory

The Wechsler Memory Scale (WMS) (Wechsler, 1945) samples several memory functions. It has seven subtests: Personal and Current Information, Orientation, Mental Control, Logical Memory, Digit Span, Visual Reproduction and Paired-Associate Learning. A factor-analytic study (Kear-Caldwell, 1973) suggested that Paired-Associate Learning and Logical Memory measure specific memory functions. Accordingly, these two subtests were used in the study. Alternate form (A, B, C) and test–retest reliabilities for logical memory are high (Withers & Hinton, 1971; Prigatano, 1978).

The Logical Memory subscale of the WMS consists of two short paragraphs of approximately equal length, subdivided into 22 and 24 ideational units, comprised of 1 to 5 word segments delineated by a slash (/). A number of parallel forms were devised for weekly testing.

The patient was told that a passage of 4 to 5 lines would be read aloud and he should recall as much of the total paragraph as possible. The first selection was then read. After a brief pause, the subject was asked to respond. The number of ideational units recalled was noted on the test form. This procedure was then repeated for the second paragraph, and the average of the two scores was taken. No practice trial was provided.

(b) Paired-Associate Learning

The Paired-Associates Learning Test (Wechsler, 1945) was selected to assess complex verbal learning because: (a) it is sensitive to cognitive deterioration in depressive syndromes; (b) it incorporates a typical 'hold' test of neuropsychological function, which usually does not show deterioration after brain damage; and (c) it provides an individualized control for the difficulty level of the items to be learned.

The patient was informed that the examiner would read out a list of words, two at a time and that he was expected to remember which words went together. The sample of EAST-WEST, GOLD-SILVER was given and the experimenter would say, 'And if I say the word GOLD, you would naturally say (pause) SILVER'. When it was clear that the patient fully understood the task, 10 consecutive word-pairs were read aloud at the rate of one pair every two seconds. Following the last word-pair, a 5-second interval was allowed before testing for recall. The subject was then asked to recall the second word of each pair as the first word only was reread aloud.

Feedback was given in the form of 'That's right' or 'No', as either a right or wrong answer was given. Six word-pairs were seen as non-competitive (easy), while four were competitive (hard). Patients were assured that if they could not remember any word(s) the first time, 'don't worry, there will be other words read to you again, and so on, until you can remember more of them.' The score was the number of word-pairs recalled up to a maximum of 10. Ten equivalent versions were used to allow for the possibility that improvements in memory performance may have resulted from practice with the task rather than the recovery of verbal learning ability. Patients were tested every week.

4. Symptom Card Sort (SCS–65)

The Symptom Card Sort (SCS–65) is a self-report rating oriented toward the symptomatic behaviour of psychiatric patients. The item-pool for this scale was derived from a number of existing sources, namely, the Hopkins Symptom Checklist (Derogatis, Rickels, & Rock, 1976); the Pilowsky Depression Questionnaire (Pilowsky & Spalding, 1972); the Newcastle study (Carney, Roth & Garside, 1965); and two factor-analytic studies of the Symptom Checklist (SCL) (Lipman, Chase, Rickels, Covi, Derogatis, & Uhlenhuth, 1969; Williams, Lipman, Rickels, Covi, Uhlenhuth, & Mattson, 1968). Based on the earlier factor analyses with a large sample of 1,115 psychiatric patients, five clinically relevant factors were isolated: Somatization, General Neurotic Feelings, Cognitive-Performance Difficulty, Depression, and Fear-Anxiety. From the full scale of about ninety items, a subset of 29 were chosen from the Hopkins Symptom Distress Checklist (HSDC). Using these 29 items and an additional 36 from the two other sources given, in all, 65 items were selected to provide a comprehensive coverage of the patients' foci of distress. The sixty-five items included the highest loading items from each of the major syndromes identified: depression (11 items), anxiety (8 items), somatic (12 items), anger (7 items), memory deficits (7 items), cognitive disturbance (9 items), self-concept (4 items), and guilt (7 items).

The patient was shown a yellow-coloured, 20 inch × 8 inch strip of cardboard on which had been printed, in bold type, six categories, from left to right labelled 'not at all', 'once in a while', 'sometimes', 'often', 'very often' and 'all the time'. Directly below each heading was an empty space of approximately 10 cm × 8 cm for entering the Q-Sort items. Patients were informed that the self-ratings should refer to how they perceive their personal circumstances at the present time ('how you feel or think of yourself at this moment').

The independently sorted Q items in the SCS–65 were thus placed along a 6-point continuum of adjustment prior to treatment, during each week of hospitalization, and at the post-treatment phase. The severity score reflected the relative position of each Q item among all the other Q items on a continuum of adjustment for every patient, week by week.

The cards were shuffled each time before being placed randomly before the patient. One week later, again at approximately the same time of day, the patients were retested using the same procedure.

5. Mood and sleep ratings

For our investigation, 16 bipolar pairs were adopted from the previous work of Bond and Lader (1974) and another 12 were chosen specifically to measure the emotional and cognitive concerns of hospitalized depressives. Patients were told that their moods would be monitored by the investigator, using line scales. The Visual Mood Analogue Scale (VMAS) and the procedure for filling it out were then explained. The 28 item-pairs were arranged randomly on a single sheet of paper, each pair separated by a 100 millimetre line. Under the heading, a set of instructions was printed. The subject was instructed to respond to each adjective-pair according to how he or she felt 'right now' by marking across the line.

Three visual analogue scales of 100 mm each were used for sleep ratings referring respectively to 'getting off to sleep' (very quick–very slow), 'quality of sleep' (very bad–very good) and 'feeling on wakening' (very sleepy–very alert). These items were included on a separate form. To ensure independence of rating patients were told not to look back at their earlier ratings.

Patients each received a week's supply of VMAS forms arranged in order. They were instructed to fill out the VMAS form sometime during the designated time period every second day. If that was not possible, they were to indicate the time of day it was filled out. Each week, the mood forms were collected and a further weeks' supply issued. Thus, each patient completed a mood and sleep scale every other day over a minimum 28-day period.

DRUGS

After admission to hospital, most patients were given drugs. Typically, these drugs were tricyclic antidepressants, such as amitriptyline or imipramine. The initial daily dosage for each patient generally reflected the severity of illness: typically, 50–75 mg/day for mild depression, 75–100 mg/day for moderate depression and 100–150 mg/day for severe depression. If neither improvement nor unwanted side effects supervened, the dosage was usually increased gradually to a maximum of 225 mg/day. The drug was changed or dosage adjusted by the various medical registrars assigned to the in-patient wards. These changes were independent of our monitoring. No formal psychotherapy was given except simple support.

Anti-anxiety medication (for example, diazepam, range: 5–10 mg/day) and hypnotics (for example, nitrazepam, range: 5–10 mg at night) were generally needed (46 and 58 patients, respectively). Twelve patients were not given antidepressants but only night sedation for insomnia, or anti-anxiety drugs.

ANALYSIS OF DATA

Because this was an open clinical investigation, patients could not be kept in the study for a specified period, being treated from 4 to 12 weeks, with some even longer. Thus a multiple variable baseline design across behavioural and somatic features, mood states, and cognitive functioning was used to evaluate the relationships between these aspects of depression. Patients had to be placed in terms of weekly treatment blocks, corresponding to the period that they remained in hospital. Several computer programs suggested by Nie and co-workers (1975) were used to analyse the average mood, symptom, and cognitive change scores for each patient. The Scatterplot program computed both the correlation of scores with time and the slope of the regression line. As the variability of each adjective scale differed between patients, variability within patients, over occasions, and among measurement variables was examined, using univariate t tests for continuous variables and chi-square for categorical variables. Because a few mood measures showed extremes of range, a $\log_e (x + 1)$ transformation was applied to the individual scores to normalize the distribution.

The initial large-scale parametric, comparative analysis used was a one-way multivariate analysis of variance (MANOVA) of the mood self-ratings, symptom Q-Sort, and perceptual-motor tests analysed separately over time. A one-way analysis of variance (ANOVA) was performed on the symptom data of the first four weeks for the total patient group, then for the decreasing sample size. Additional comparisons between-weeks were made for the symptom data, using the Wilcoxon matched-pairs, signed-ranks test.

Within-patient correlations were calculated for those symptom measures with significant 'sensitivity' to treatment over time and also between the symptoms and mood self-ratings found sensitive to the ward programme. Symptom differences among patients were also compared by ANCOVA, using the pretreatment symptom value as the covariate. When a covariance F-ratio revealed a significant mood difference beyond the 0.05 level, a within-subject analysis was carried out to ascertain how many patients were involved.

The changes over time for each major mood, symptom, and performance (both cognitive and motor) measure were plotted out for each patient separately, then for the total group to identify any consistent patterning between variables. Parametric analyses of variance and, where appropriate, covariance were carried out, changes over time being estimated against between-occasion, within-subject error variance. To examine further the time courses, orthogonal analyses of trend were computed based on the polynomial coefficient. Such a procedure assumes that the variables are equally spaced on some dimension and makes no assumptions concerning variance-covariance structure.

Separately, treatment outcome (for example, 'good' versus 'poor' clinical recovery) was examined by comparing group differences on a series of univariate t tests. A further analysis related measures of baseline psychopathology to change over treatment. Data for those patients showing a good and poor outcome were analysed in this way.

Lastly, sex differences in the frequency and expression of sad affect, cognitions and overt behaviour were sought using t-test comparisons.

4. Results

PATIENT CHARACTERISTICS

Of 87 successive admissions, 70 patients met the full admission and pre-screening criteria. Their characteristics are listed in Table 2.

DURATION OF STAY IN HOSPITAL

Five patients stayed in hospital for less than a month, the majority (46; 66 per cent) for 1–2 months and the remainder (19) for over 2 months. These groups were compared, using a one-way analysis of variance. The mean age of few short-stay patients was lower than that of the others (Table 3). Duration of stay was not related to sex. Onset was sudden in 49 patients, and usually precipitated by an identifiable cause. The highest number of cases with a slow onset (13 out of 21; $p < 0.001$) fell in the medium-stay category. Of the 10 patients who reported no former episode prior to their index admission, 8 remained in hospital for up to two months. Eighteen patients had a history of 3 or more previous affective episodes; 6 of these were re-admitted within 6 months. Recurrence was not related to age at onset nor to severity of illness.

All but 6 patients reported that their current affective illness had lasted more than a month; the median duration was 3 months. Only 3 patients had been free of symptoms for the previous year. In general, the longer the duration of affective symptoms the longer the time spent in hospital.

Sixty-one of the patients identified a precipitating factor. The 9 patients who had difficulty identifying a life stress were more likely to be classed as endogenously depressed and to have a worse prognosis.

Forty-seven (67 per cent) of the patients had a history of self-injury or attempted suicide. Twelve patients had made at least one attempt and four had made several. At interview nearly 90 per cent of patients admitted to experiencing mild-to-frequent suicidal

Table 2. *Characteristics of 70 hospitalized depressives at admission*

Variable	Male ($N = 28$)		Female ($N = 42$)	
	Number	Per cent	Number	Per cent
General				
Age				
20–29	6	9	11	16
30–39	11	16	16	23
40–49	4	6	5	7
50 and over	7	10	10	14
Marital status				
Married	12	17	22	31
Single	8	11	13	19
Divorced	2	3	3	4
Widowed	2	3	1	1
Separated	4	6	3	4
Race				
White	28	40	40	57
Non-white	0	–	2	3
Occupational status				
I Professional	2	3	1	1
II Managerial	2	3	4	6
III White collar	3	4	9	13
IV Tradesmen	13	19	6	9
V Semi-skilled workers	6	9	12	17
VI Unskilled workers	0	–	1	1
VII Students	2	3	3	4
Employment status				
Employed	12	17	10	14
Not employed	16	23	32	46
Illness				
Diagnostic category				
Unipolar	20	29	33	47
Bipolar	1	1	1	1
Endogenous	2	3	5	7
Psychotic	5	7	3	4

Table 2. *Cont.*

Variable	Male ($N = 28$)		Female ($N = 42$)	
	Number	Per cent	Number	Per cent
Age at onset of current depressive episode				
Before 20	3	6	5	10
20–29	8	11	17	24
30–39	9	13	9	13
40–49	3	4	5	7
50 and over	5	7	6	9
Duration of present illness				
Less than 1 month	3	4	3	4
1–2 months	13	19	20	29
3 months–1 year	11	16	17	24
Over 1 year	1	1	2	3
Number of previous episodes				
0	4	6	6	9
1	8	11	14	20
2	8	11	12	17
3	5	7	6	9
4	1	1	2	3
5 or more	2	3	2	3
Number of previous admissions				
0	10	14	6	9
1	13	19	28	40
2	2	3	3	4
3	1	1	2	3
4	0	–	2	3
5 or more	2	3	1	1
Background				
Family history (13 male; 23 female)				
Neurotic	7	10	8	11
Depressive	5	7	10	14
Alcoholic	1	1	1	1
Schizophrenic	0	–	3	4
Phobic	0	–	1	1

Note: Housewives were classified according to their own occupation before marriage.

Table 3. *Background of patients and length of hospitalization*

Variable	Length of stay		
	Short	Medium	Long
	(Up to 1 month) (*N* = 5)	(1–2 months) (*N* = 46)	(Over 2 months) (*N* = 19)
Mean age			
Male	27	39	36
Female	24	41	40
Sex			
Male	2	17	9
Female	3	29	10
Type of onset			
Clearly sudden	4	33	12
Slowly insidious	1	13	7
Previous episodes			
0	1	7	2
1	2	15	5
2	1	12	7
3 or more	1	12	5
Clinical course of present episode			
Steadily deteriorating	0	1	1
No amelioration after onset	1	2	2
No amelioration after incomplete improvement	1	5	3
Steadily improving	2	34	11
Fluctuating	1	4	2

thoughts prior to the index admission. Two female patients made one or more attempts at self-mutilation during their current admission.

HAMILTON RATING SCALE FOR DEPRESSION

The mean total Hamilton Depression Scale scores diminished successively at each weekly evaluation and analysis of covariance, using

Table 3. *Cont.*

Variable	Length of stay		
	Short	Medium	Long
	(Up to 1 month) (*N* = 5)	(1–2 months) (*N* = 46)	(Over 2 months) (*N* = 19)
Duration of present episode			
less than 1 month	2	4	0
1 month–3 months	2	24	7
3 months–1 year	1	17	10
greater than 1 year	0	1	2
Precipitating factor			
Yes	5	41	15
No	0	5	4
Age at onset			
Before 20	1	5	2
20–29	3	16	6
30–39	1	11	6
40–49	0	5	3
50 and over	0	9	2
Positive family history			
Yes	3	18	11
No	2	28	8
Previous suicide attempts			
0	3	33	11
1	2	7	3
2	0	4	3
3 or more	0	2	2

the initial scores as the covariate, showed that the reduction was highly significant by the end of the study ($p < 0.001$; Table 4). Global severity was initially moderately severe and fell progressively to within the mild range after the sixth week ($p < 0.001$).

The mean Hamilton values before treatment, and at 21 and 42 days of treatment are plotted in Fig. 1. All the constituent ratings, except somatic symptoms (gastro-intestinal), genito-urinary complaints, paranoid beliefs, and obsessionality were improved by

Table 4. *Hamilton ratings and Global Severity ratings at weekly intervals*

		Week of rating						
Total group	N	On admission 70	1 70	2 70	3 70	4 65	5 60	6 56
Total								
Hamilton R.S.	Mean (SD)	36.0 (9.6)	32.8 (11.5)	29.8 (12.0)	24.6 (13.5)	18.6 (13.9)	12.9 (13.3)	10.7* (13.5)
Global Severity**	Mean (SD)	3.8 (1.0)	3.7 (1.0)	2.8 (1.1)	2.1 (1.2)	1.9 (1.1)	1.5 (1.2)	1.3* (1.3)

*$p < 0.001$ analysis of covariance
**Scoring: 0: Not present   4: Moderately severe
1: Very mild   5: Severe
2: Mild   6: Extremely severe
3: Moderate

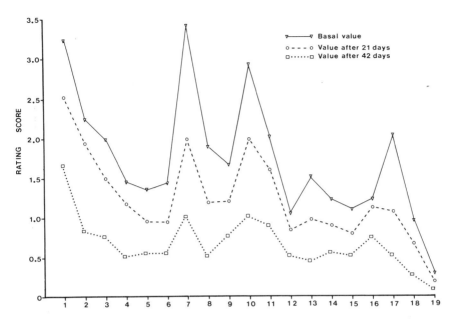

Fig. 1. Symptom profiles of 70 depressed patients on Hamilton Depression Scale before, and after 21 days, and after 42 days of treatment.

1 = depressed mood (rated 0–4); 2 = suicide (0–4); 3 = guilt (0–4); 4 = initial insomnia (0–2); 5 = middle insomnia (2); 6 = delayed insomnia (2); 7 = work and interests (4); 8 = retardation (4); 9 = agitation (2); 10 = psychic anxiety (4); 11 = somatic anxiety (4); 12 = gastrointestinal symptoms (2); 13 = general somatic symptoms (2); 14 = hypochondriasis (4); 15 = loss of insight (2); 16 = genital symptoms (2); 17 = depersonalization (4); 18 = paranoid symptoms (4); 19 = obsessional syptoms (2).

treatment. The last was negligible at the start. Weight (not shown) which was recorded at weekly intervals by a nurse, increased only just significantly ($F1,69 = 4.35; p < 0.05$).

Three of the 21 Hamilton symptoms were specially marked upon admission, but changed dramatically by the end of the treatment. For example, the first symptom, depressed mood, decreased by 50 per cent ($F1,69 = 14.65; p < 0.001$). Similarly, the seventh variable, inability to work, had improved remarkably by the time of discharge.

Psychic anxiety was of major concern for most patients, since it caused them to restrict their normal activities. Although treatment lessened such anxiety ($F1,69 = 12.78; p < 0.01$), many patients continued to worry needlessly about trivia. The fourth highest symptom, depersonalization and derealization, was first rated as moderately disturbing, with patients reporting at times 'feeling out of touch with their surroundings'. After therapy this symptom declined to 0.5 (out of 2), indicating only occasional feelings of unreality ($F = 6.30$; $p < 0.02$).

Among eight Hamilton items falling within the 0–2 scoring range, only three – agitation, insomnia, and general somatic symptoms – were high. All were significantly reduced by the time of post-treatment evaluation.

PERFORMANCE TASKS

As Table 5, shows, tapping rate, symbol copying, digit symbol substitution, and Gibson Spiral Maze time all improved during the first few weeks and then reached a plateau (analysis of covariance, initial values as covariate). However, the average error score for the Gibson Spiral Maze declined slowly with a significant linear trend. Most patients were not 'quick-and-careless' or 'slow-and-careless'; rather they were 'slow-and-accurate'. About 14 patients continued to make errors over the weeks, apparently concentrating on speed rather than accuracy.

Wechsler Memory Scale

(a) Logical memory

Baseline recall was quite poor for many patients (Table 5), on average only about a quarter of total content of two paragraphs. Even at the final week patients could only recall two-thirds of the material comprising paragraph 1, and 58 per cent of paragraph 2. Though a practice effect cannot be totally discounted, the use of alternate forms and the failure to return to normal levels suggests that any such learning was minimal.

(b) Paired-associate learning

Unlike logical memory, the only significant increase for easy word-pair performance was from baseline to week 1. A ceiling effect for the easy word-pairs was attained at about the fourth week (mean = 5.8, maximum = 6).

The more difficult word-pairs showed no significant improvement after the third week.

SYMPTOM CARD SORT (SCS–65)

A one-way analysis of variance (ANOVA) was performed on each of the 65 items in the Symptom Card Sort (SCS–65) comparing the values before and after treatment for each item separately. Using the baseline ratings as the covariate, adjusted mean changes were tested for statistical significance between weeks by univariate *t*-tests (Table 6). The week for which (a) the first and (b) the most significant shift occurred are also given.

As patients recover, all 11 items in the *depression* cluster improved. All except two had significantly improved by the fourth week in hospital. Out of all 12 *somatic indices*, only 4 altered, probably because initial values were already low. Early reductions were only distinct for dry mouth, feeling worse in mornings, and slowed movements. Most somatic concomitants of depression lessen within three weeks of treatment.

With the *anxiety* factor, the bodily signs of anxiety disappear first, followed by a reduction in anticipatory or mental anxiety. On a cognitive level, some patients continue to be fearful of certain situations or people. Of clinical interest, the three most severe items all relate to anxiety, with 'I worry a lot' ranking highest.

Recovery of deficits in *concentration* and immediate memory recall was similarly impressive. Only one item, 'mind goes blank', did not reach significance. Ability to concentrate improved early in treatment whereas subjective difficulties in retrieving material from short-term memory storage persisted longer. Since difficulty in focusing on, or paying attention to events is more prominent that the patients' difficulty in recalling material from long-term memory, the observed deficit is likely to be one of 'registration'.

The fact that memory improvement, as tested experimentally, is almost immediate is inconsistent with patients' reports that their memory problems recover slowly. However, performance tests measure memory recall of a short paragraph, whereas patients' self-ratings on the Q-Sort refer to different concerns. Patients often complain that they cannnot remember a name, telephone number,

Table 5. *Effect of treatment on performance tests*

Scores (SD)	On admission	Week of treatment 1	2	3	4	5	6
Tapping rate/30s							
Mean (SD)	83.5 (22.1)	96.6 (21.2)	104.3 (19.7)	110.4 (19.7)	114.4 (19.7)	116.0 (18.0)	117.1 (19.1)
p-values < (between weeks)		0.001	0.001	0.001	0.025	N.S.	N.S.
Symbol Copying Test (number copied/90s)							
Mean (SD)	74.5 (26.4)	79.3 (27.2)	89.4 (28.4)	97.4 (29.4)	105.1 (30.0)	111.0 (28.8)	113.1 (28.4)
p-values < (between weeks)		0.001	0.001	0.001	0.019	N.S.	N.S.
Digit Symbol Substitution Test (Number coded/90s)							
Mean (SD)	32.7 (12.9)	34.3 (11.6)	38.6 (12.5)	42.2 (12.0)	45.1 (12.8)	50.5 (12.7)	51.8 (12.9)
p-values < (between weeks)		0.028	0.001	0.001	0.001	0.001	N.S.
Gibson Spiral Maze Time (in seconds)							
Mean (SD)	110.2 (79.6)	104.3 (76.9)	85.7 (46.8)	75.8 (30.1)	71.3 (23.9)	70.2 (21.6)	68.6 (20.6)
p-values < (between weeks)		0.001	0.001	0.016	0.001	N.S.	N.S.

Gibson Spiral Maze
(No. of errors)

Mean (SD)	3.1 (2.5)	2.9 (2.3)	2.3 (1.5)	2.0 (2.0)	1.4 (1.3)	1.2 (0.9)	1.3 (0.6)
p-values < (between weeks)	0.05	0.06	0.02	N.S.	N.S.	N.S.	

Logical memory
(Paragraph 1)
(Maximum score 22)

Mean (SD)	6.5 (3.1)	7.5 (3.5)	9.9 (3.8)	11.8 (3.8)	13.0 (4.3)	14.9 (4.5)	14.8 (4.7)
p-values < (between weeks)	0.01	0.01	0.01	0.02	0.04	N.S.	

Logical memory
(Paragraph 2)
(Maximum score 24)

Mean (SD)	5.6 (2.4)	6.0 (2.9)	8.8 (3.3)	10.0 (3.7)	12.0 (4.2)	13.3 (4.4)	13.9 (4.7)
p-values < (between weeks)	0.01	0.01	0.01	0.01	0.03	N.S.	

Paired-associates
(*Easy*)
(Maximum score 6)

Mean (SD)	4.3 (1.0)	4.9 (1.1)	5.4 (0.9)	5.5 (1.1)	5.8 (0.4)	6.0 (0.6)	5.8 (0.5)
p-values < (between weeks)	0.01	N.S.	N.S.	N.S.	N.S.	N.S.	

Paired-assoiates
(*Hard*)
(maximum score 4)

Mean (SD)	0.7 (1.0)	0.7 (1.1)	1.3 (1.3)	1.8 (1.4)	2.1 (1.3)	2.4 (1.2)	2.7 (1.3)
p-values < (between weeks)	N.S.	0.01	0.02	N.S.	N.S.	N.S.	

location of a personal possession, the details of a book or newspaper just read, facts about people they know or what they were about to say before some interruption.

Feelings of *guilt* decrease slowly, and not before the fifth week. In particular the intropunitive component (i.e., 'I punish myself') shows delayed recovery.

With respect to *cognitive* factors, patients become more decisive but expect more out of life than they have put into it. Self-reports of *anger* wane after a four- to six-week period in hospital. Excluded from this general trend is self-directed anger and criticism of others.

Self-concept was tapped by four items: three were positively keyed (likeable, nice, or worthwhile person) and one negatively ('I feel inferior'). Mean values for the three positively-worded statements either remained constant or rose only slightly: patients are slow to adopt a positive self-view. On the other hand, feelings of inferiority changed significantly during the fifth week.

SPEED OF RECOVERY OF DEPRESSIVE SYMPTOMS

The data in Table 6 can be re-evaluated by examining the items which improve at various times. Thus, 11 symptoms declined rapidly and significantly over the first two weeks in hospital and included depression, bodily anxiety, and somatic discomfort. Of particular importance were items measuring suicidal thinking, hopelessness, and diminished interest in life.

Three of the five symptoms which decreased in frequency from week 2 to 3 (time passes slowly, cannot make a decision, cannot sleep at night) were more troublesome than the two remaining symptoms.

From the third to fourth week, eight additional symptoms declined significantly, such as feeling angry, lonely, or bored. The level of bodily anxiety also fell.

Some variables only improved after one month or more. Between weeks 4 and 5, 12 features of depression remitted. Shifts in anger, anxiety, and guilt were prominent at this juncture, with some associated cognitive disturbance. An increase in sexual arousal was also noted.

A further 7 symptoms diminished significantly by the final self-rating. At this time, patients seemed more willing to acknowledge how they truly felt. Only during the sixth week did the cognitive component of patients' anxiety actually subside. Of all the 65 items comprising the Q-Sort, "I worry a lot" had the highest pre-treatment intensity and frequency of occurrence, and showed the slowest rate of remission.

Twelve symptoms did not change, partly because of their low level of severity on admission. Even at final assessment patients did not view themselves as nice, likeable, or worthwhile. Also, coming into hospital does not help patients to alter their self-perceived level of intropunitive anger.

Though no consistent pattern of remission emerged for item-clusters used to define the major features of depression, somatic symptoms usually changed during the early phase of treatment, by the first to third week. Depressed mood was significantly reduced, even absent for some patients by the fourth week of in-patient care, with short-term memory deficits showing somewhat differential rates of recovery ranging from weeks 3 to 6.

MOOD PROFILES

Changes over time

The analyses of mood ratings are presented in Table 7. Nine variables failed to change significantly, of which two fell just short of the required significance level (chatty–quiet (20) and afraid–not afraid (23)). Three other measures produced a linear trend which just reached significance: sociability (14), well liked (25), and want to get well (28).

The most significant linear function was achieved for self-regard (24) followed by happy–sad (11) and cheerful–depressed (17). Next was the rating 'life is hopeless' (22), with both a significant linear and quadratic trend.

Following this, significance of symptom reduction for factors relating to arousal is greater than that for remaining factors of psychopathology: tense–relaxed (9), attentive–dreamy (10), alert–drowsy (1), getting off to sleep (29) and strong–feeble (3). In general, trends were linear with a quadratic (curvilinear) component in only three variables (3, 9, and 22).

Of the 9 measures unaffected by treatment three related to clinical depression, these being afraid (23), quality of sleep (30),

Table 6. *Differential rates of recovery for Symptom Card Sort items*

Symptom item stem	Pre-treatment	Post-treatment	Difference (+ or −)	p value	First significant shift — Weeks in hospital 1	2	3	4	5	6	Linear trend	No change
Depression												
I feel lonely	3.30	2.23	−1.07	0.001				x				
Time passes slowly	3.40	2.33	−1.07	0.001			x					
Future is hopeless	3.58	2.00	−1.58	0.001	x							
I feel bored	3.23	1.96	−1.27	0.001				x				
I cry easily	2.77	1.75	−1.02	0.001					x			
No interest in life	3.84	2.21	−1.63	0.001	x		o					
Suicidal thoughts	2.46	1.71	−0.75	0.005	x							
Sexual arousal	1.33	1.95	+0.62	0.01					x			
Poor appetite	3.01	1.71	−1.30	0.001	x							
I hide my true feelings	3.40	2.58	−0.82	0.01							x	
I neglect my appearance	2.61	1.46	−1.15	0.001	x							
Somatic												
Mouth dry or coated	3.73	2.31	−1.42	0.001	x							
Gastric distress	1.35	1.15	−0.20	−								−
Difficulty breathing	1.75	1.50	−0.25	−								−
Early morning awakening	2.98	1.77	−1.21	0.001					x			
Weight loss	1.94	1.21	−0.71	0.01							x	

Back and chest pains	1.48	1.29	−0.19	—							—
Bowel trouble	1.72	1.41	−0.31	—							—
Cannot sleep at night	3.38	2.23	−1.15	0.001		x					
Arms/legs feel heavy	2.37	1.35	−1.02	0.001	x					x	
Feel worse in AM	3.35	2.15	−1.20	0.001	x						
Feel worse in PM	2.65	1.77	−0.88	0.01	x					x	
Slowed movements	3.50	2.03	−1.47	0.001	x						
Anxiety											
Nervous or shaky	3.81	2.65	−1.16	0.001				x			
I avoid people, situations	3.61	2.60	−1.01	0.001		x					
Trembling a lot	3.17	2.06	−1.13	0.001		x					
Perspire profusely	2.75	1.85	−0.90	0.007	x						
Rapid heart palpitations	2.88	1.83	−1.05	0.001	x						
Physically tense	3.71	2.73	−0.98	0.001		x					
I feel panicky	3.85	2.61	−1.24	0.001		x					
I worry a lot	4.36	3.21	−1.15	0.001						x	
Memory											
Trouble remembering	2.98	2.12	−0.86	0.001					x		
Trouble concentrating	3.81	2.75	−1.06	0.001	x						
Mind goes blank	2.32	1.81	−0.51	—							
I have a poor memory	2.85	1.79	−1.06	0.004				x			
I cannot pay attention	3.71	2.38	−1.33	0.001				x			
Forget where things put	2.35	1.56	−0.79	0.009			x				
Forget what people say	2.79	2.11	−0.68	0.01							

Table 6. *Cont.*

Symptom item stem	Pre-treatment	Post-treatment	Difference (+ or −)	P value	Weeks in hospital 1	2	3	4	5	6	Linear trend	No change
Guilt												
Committed the worst sins	1.81	0.83	−0.98	0.001				x				
Bothered by my conscience	3.17	2.11	−1.06	0.001					x			
Guilt feelings	3.35	2.48	−0.87	0.01							x	
Ashamed of my past	3.08	2.33	−0.75	0.004					x			
I've let people down	3.40	2.33	−1.07	0.001						x		
I usually blame myself	3.50	2.61	−0.89	0.01					x			
I punish myself	3.19	2.33	−0.86	0.01							x	
Cognitive												
Cannot make a decision	3.48	2.40	−1.08	0.001			x					
I never do anything right	2.90	1.98	−0.92	0.01			x					
I'm easily upset	3.00	2.13	−0.87	0.01							x	
Pass up opportunities	2.58	2.08	−0.50	—								—

	Pre	Post	Change	p						
I deserve more from life	1.88	2.33	+0.45	—						—
I give up too easily	3.08	2.38	−0.70	0.01					x	
I feel abused by people	2.69	1.71	−0.98	0.001					x	
I never disagree	2.79	1.90	−0.89	0.01				x		
Let others decide for me	2.81	1.88	−0.93	0.001			x			
Anger										
I'm angry only at myself	3.31	2.90	−0.41	—						—
I'm angry at the world	2.06	1.33	−0.73	0.01	x					
I feel angry	2.58	1.96	−0.62	0.01		x				
I'm easily angered	2.67	1.85	−0.82	0.01					x	
I lose my temper easily	2.10	1.48	−0.62	0.01		x				
I criticize other people	2.31	1.81	−0.50	—				o		
I suppress my anger	3.00	2.23	−0.77	0.007			x			
Self concept										
I feel rather inferior	3.23	2.13	−1.10	0.001		x				
I'm a likeable person	2.65	2.94	−0.29	—						—
I'm a nice person	2.65	2.98	+0.33	—						—
I'm a worthwhile person	2.46	2.98	+0.52	—						—

Note: The pre- post-treatment values reflect the mean scores for the total group ($N = 70$). Eight of the 65 variables which did not change week by week over the first six weeks did show an overall linear trend.
x denotes the first week for which a significant improvement was noted.
o denotes the week for which the most significant shift occured if different from that already shown for x.

Table 7. *Summary of trend analyses of mood profiles and sleep ratings*

Orthogonal polynomial contrasts	Mean square	f-Ratio	$p =$	
Mood profiles				
1. Alert/drowsy				
Linear	11326.04	9.686	0.003	
Quadratic	303.65	0.645	0.436	n.s.
2. Calm/excited				
Linear	5527.19	7.619	0.008	
Quadratic	154.73	0.373	0.544	n.s.
3. Strong/feeble				
Linear	10973.08	9.002	0.004	
Quadratic	1130.54	4.555	0.039	
4. Muzzy/clear-headed				
Linear	6250.21	6.821	0.016	
Quadratic	259.61	0.928	0.340	n.s.
5. Well co-ordinated/clumsy				
Linear	7446.80	6.665	0.012	
Quadratic	653.01	2.444	0.124	n.s.
6. Tired/energetic				
Linear	1981.02	2.673	0.108	n.s.
Quadratic	1221.22	3.592	0.063	n.s.
7. Troubled/tranquil				
Linear	9965.24	9.192	0.004	
Quadratic	482.24	1.094	0.301	n.s.
8. Mentally slow/quick-witted				
Linear	7312.01	8.084	0.006	
Quadratic	113.24	0.474	0.494	n.s.
9. Tense/relaxed				
Linear	10578.67	10.173	0.001	
Quadratic	1872.71	5.672	0.021	

Table 7. *Cont.*

Orthogonal polynomial contrasts	Mean square	*f*-Ratio	*p* =
10. Attentive/dreamy			
Linear	9602.60	10.145	0.003
Quadratic	181.51	0.613	0.437 n.s.
11. Happy/sad			
Linear	17378.66	17.642	0.001
Quadratic	372.09	0.703	0.406 n.s.
12. Hostile/friendly			
Linear	431.76	0.575	0.456 n.s.
Quadratic	25.87	0.061	0.806 n.s.
13. Interested/bored			
Linear	9553.33	8.917	0.004
Quadratic	1493.31	3.636	0.063 n.s.
14. Withdrawn/sociable			
Linear	3515.57	4.337	0.042
Quadratic	14.08	0.027	0.869 n.s.
15. No sexual desire/aroused			
Linear	2185.66	2.085	0.155 n.s.
Quadratic	67.34	0.182	0.671 n.s.
16. Impulsive/plan my actions			
Linear	8562.94	8.815	0.005
Quadratic	14.47	0.034	0.854 n.s.
17. Cheerful/depressed			
Linear	15268.78	13.345	0.001
Quadratic	869.61	1.716	0.197 n.s.
18. Trusting/suspicious			
Linear	2419.91	1.933	0.170 n.s.
Quadratic	94.14	0.207	0.651 n.s.

Table 7. *Cont.*

Orthogonal polynomial contrasts	Mean square	*f*-Ratio	*p* =
19. No friends/many friends			
Linear	2691.99	7.790	0.007
Quadratic	7.29	0.027	0.881 n.s.
20. Chatty/quiet			
Linear	3823.35	3.184	0.081 n.s.
Quadratic	288.88	0.525	0.472 n.s.
21. Angry/affectionate			
Linear	1177.54	0.995	0.323 n.s.
Quadratic	74.88	0.223	0.639 n.s.
22. Full of hope/no hope			
Linear	11122.59	11.844	0.001
Quadratic	2235.06	7.597	0.008
23. Afraid/not afraid			
Linear	2766.15	3.586	0.064 n.s.
Quadratic	9.13	0.025	0.887 n.s.
24. High/low self-regard			
Linear	13179.54	23.655	0.001
Quadratic	150.19	0.598	0.433 n.s.
25. Well-liked/disliked			
Linear	1586.01	4.133	0.048
Quadratic	3.70	0.198	0.888 n.s.

and loss of sexual desire (15). three hostility variables – hostile–friendly (12), trusting–suspicious (18), and irritable–good-natured (27) – also showed no change.

DIFFERENTIAL RATES OF RECOVERY

Mood changes in individual patients

The changes in mood on the self-rated analogue scales are ranked from most to least remission in Table 8. Difference scores from the

Table 7. *Cont.*

Orthogonal polynomial contrasts	Mean square	ƒ-Ratio	p =	
26. Capable/helpless				
Linear	5317.66	7.233	0.015	
Quadratic	16.89	0.526	0.819	n.s.
27. Irritable/good natured				
Linear	245.84	0.250	0.619	n.s.
Quadratic	62.66	0.112	0.737	n.s.
28. Want to get well/don't care				
Linear	2594.61	4.405	0.044	
Quadratic	60.38	0.199	0.657	n.s.
Sleep ratings				
29. Getting off to sleep				
Linear	8940.85	9.345	0.004	
Quadratic	36.06	0.090	0.765	n.s.
30. Quality of sleep				
Linear	1783.96	2.066	0.157	n.s.
Quadratic	1810.10	2.294	0.136	n.s.
31. Feeling on wakening				
Linear	5497.63	7.015	0.010	
Quadratic	22.83	0.055	0.815	n.s.

baseline to final evaluation and the week in which the first significant drop in intensity occurred were calculated separately for each patient.

The two scales describing feelings of depression show initial high levels with greatest improvement. Notwithstanding, 15 and 19 patients, respectively, showed no significant amelioration on these scales. Rapid recovery was apparent for about half the patients with respect to feelings of feebleness and drowsiness: by the third week, ratings had declined by 46 and 47 per cent, respectively.

On three measures relating to mental control, overall recovery was good. Thirty patients felt more lucid, attentive and mentally

Table 8. *Comparison of the differential rates of recovery with amount of mood change*

Mood self-rating (code no.)	Pre-treatment mean	Mean at discharge	Mean difference (+ or −)	p value	Rate of improvement[1]						
					Time in weeks for 70 patients[2]						
					Fast		Moderate		Slow		No change
					0–1	1–2	2–3	3–4	4–5	5–6	
1. Cheerful/depressed (17)	73.85	40.32	−33.43	0.01	0	27	9	4	7	8	15
2. Happy/sad (11)	72.98	40.31	−32.67	0.01	1	23	12	6	3	6	19
3. Strong/feeble (3)	62.62	34.90	−27.72	0.01	0	18	16	12	4	4	16
4. Full of hope/no hope (22)	57.06	30.60	−26.46	0.01	1	21	16	7	4	6	15
5. Capable/helpless (26)	58.27	32.13	−26.14	0.01	0	18	12	5	9	5	21
6. Interested/bored (13)	62.92	36.83	−26.09	0.01	0	19	16	1	5	4	25
7. Alert/drowsy (1)	54.71	29.04	−25.67	0.01	0	20	11	9	7	3	20
8. Troubled/tranquil (7)	21.15	46.79	+25.64	0.01	0	11	16	12	1	8	22
9. Mentally slow/quick-witted (8)	39.06	64.25	+25.19	0.01	0	7	24	9	9	3	18
10. High/low self-regard (24)	67.96	43.60	−24.36	0.01	0	15	19	5	5	5	21
11. Impulsive/plan my actions (16)	37.96	61.25	+23.29	0.01	0	11	18	8	5	7	27
12. Muzzy/clear-headed (4)	44.79	67.83	+23.04	0.01	0	15	18	7	5	1	24

13. Tense/relaxed (9)	20.67	43.38	+22.71	0.01	0	7	16	8	1	7	31
14. Attentive/dreamy (10)	52.83	30.42	−22.41	0.01	0	19	12	11	7	6	15
15. Chatty/quiet (20)	63.83	41.58	−22.25	0.01	0	14	14	4	4	6	24
16. Well co-ordinated/clumsy (5)	48.42	26.63	−21.79	0.01	1	18	17	10	3	2	19
17. Tired/energetic (6)	32.81	49.75	−16.94	0.01	0	3	15	7	4	8	33
18. Withdrawn/sociable (14)	41.24	57.90	+16.66	0.01	0	16	13	9	7	5	20
19. Well-liked/disliked (25)	44.04	29.50	−15.54	0.01	0	17	7	1	7	6	32
20. Trusting/suspicious (18)	51.44	36.19	−15.25	0.01	0	12	16	3	9	4	26
21. Calm/excited (2)	52.15	39.10	−13.05	0.01	0	16	15	9	4	0	26
22. No sexual desire/aroused (15)	17.56	30.56	+13.00	0.01	0	13	13	4	5	8	27
23. Afraid/not afraid (23)	29.10	41.21	+12.11	0.01	0	5	12	8	9	5	31
24. Want to get well/don't care (28)	27.83	16.09	−11.74	0.03	1	15	12	3	3	1	25
25. Angry/affectionate (21)	44.10	55.75	+11.65	0.03	0	15	11	10	6	4	24
26. No friends/many friends (19)	46.81	58.31	+11.50	0.02	0	5	20	6	5	1	33
27. Irritable/good-natured (27)	44.62	55.58	+10.96	0.05	0	9	12	7	1	5	36
28. Hostile/friendly (12)	45.10	53.17	+8.07	n.s.	0	4	18	9	5	5	29

[1] The values shown for the three categories (fast, moderate, and slow) represent the subjects who first improved in that period.
[2] The data analyses are based on a series of univariate t tests (two-tailed), individual scatterplots and a chi-square analysis comparing frequencies in the three collapsed categories for rate of clinical recovery.

quicker after three weeks in hospital. After six more weeks, one-third of all patients still complained of experiencing muddled thought, 18 had difficulty in thinking clearly, and 15 remained dreamy.

Differences between patients were great. Thirty-five patients regained a renewed interest in life by the third week, data congruent with the Symptom Check List results. The individual scatterplot analyses show that 25 patients retained their feelings of mild boredom.

Twenty-four patients did not become any more talkative. A similar pattern emerges for withdrawal, since 20 patients reported no decrease in their avoidance of social contact. The 'Tiredness' factor, possibly a tricyclic side effect, remitted rather slowly, with 33 patients remaining fatigued at the end of testing.

The tendency to act without thinking, a problem for some patients, decreased by a mean 55 per cent from the baseline intensity. The intensity of feelings of hostility showed least clinical improvement. Recovery from depressive mood was, however, matched by a change in direction of hostility from highly intropunitive to normal. The irritability and hostility both change relatively slowly and are not closely related to the recovery pattern of depressed mood.

Patients were not grossly impaired in terms of how well-thought-of they were. Perceptions of how disliked patients feel seem less relevant than their own self-dislike. Many patients maintained a positive outlook or expectation of becoming well which did not appreciably affect other emotional states, which continued to fluctuate markedly. Though about 25 patients were at or near asymptote on this factor, 27 of the 45 with improved status changed during the early phase of psychiatric treatment.

Manifest and cognitive anxiety recover slowly. Indeed, 30 or so patients continued to experience both physical tension and mental anxiety prior to discharge. By this time, most patients including some with significant improvement still rated themselves on the negative side of the variables.

Moods which shift early in treatment generally change most: feelings of depression, boredom, hopelessness, low self-regard, helplessness, muddled thinking, and reluctance to engage in conversation. As the mean mood scale reduction from intake to discharge falls below 20 mm, the recovery period required takes longer for many patients.

The fact that certain patients fail to experience a more stable mood pattern does not imply that they continue to feel unwell on all measures. Their self-evaluation is not negative in every respect and even patients who developed a relatively normal mood profile showed some deviation from time to time. Despite the fact that anxiety and depression were of similar severity for most patients upon admission, their rate of recovery differed in terms of the number of patients with an improved or unimproved discharge status.

On the self-esteem dimension, 49 patients rated themselves as favourably improved; 21 subjects felt that no significant shift had occurred after admission. The negative aspect of this finding is partly consistent with the Q-Sort results that indicated that the patients' self-view is not readily enhanced.

In general, patients feel moderately but not completely helpless. For perceived helplessness there is a positive and significant shift for 49 patients. Again, the rate of improvement varies from patient to patient. Examination of the relationship of self-regard to feelings of personal helplessness reveals that the pattern of recovery of these two variables is quite similar over the various periods. A high correlation was seen between these two factors (0.76, $p < 0.001$). However, many other mood and cognitive changes on psychometric measures do not proceed hand in hand according to a nice theoretical paradigm. Curves in individual cases may be asynchronous or there may be no effect on one measure, even though the others change significantly.

BASELINE SEVERITY AND FINAL OUTCOME

In order to answer some of these points about which dimensions of mood changed most, a separate breakdown is presented of the recovery rates for patients showing a good or poor outcome (Table 9). The pattern of change is complicated by the differences in level of initial psychopathology.

When first admitted to hospital, members of the two outcome groups are largely undifferentiated on specific indices like excitability (2), troubled state (7), tension (9), hostility (12), anxiety (7) and irritability (27). Of these, the largest discrepancy scores occurred for irritability (-16.7), followed by bodily tension (-13.6). Both favoured the good improvers.

Table 9. *Comparison of amount of mood change from the pre-treatment severity level for 23 patients with good and 25 patients with poor treatment outcome*

	Good outcome N = 23			Poor outcome N = 25			2–1
	Pre-	Post-	Diff (1)	Pre-	Post-	Diff (2)	
1. Alert/drowsy	40.8	22.0	18.8	64.4	34.2	30.1	+11.3
2. Calm/excited	52.9	34.0	18.9	55.4	46.0	9.4	−9.5
3. Strong/feeble	49.8	23.8	26.0	66.4	39.3	27.1	+1.1
4. Muzzy/clear-headed	59.7	74.3	25.4	34.1	62.0	28.0	+1.6
5. Well co-ordinated/clumsy	41.5	22.3	19.2	55.4	31.4	24.0	+4.8
6. Tired/energetic	40.5	55.1	14.6	27.5	44.7	17.2	+2.6
7. Troubled/tranquil	21.2	54.6	33.3	18.3	40.8	22.5	−10.9
8. Mentally slow/quick-witted	49.3	71.8	22.5	33.7	61.3	27.6	+5.0
9. Tense/relaxed	22.3	51.9	29.7	17.1	33.2	16.0	−13.6
10. Attentive/dreamy	42.0	23.8	18.2	60.2	35.6	24.6	+6.4

11. Happy/sad	59.0	30.5	28.4	78.2	48.7	29.5	+1.0
12. Hostile/friendly	55.7	68.8	13.1	53.2	58.0	4.8	−8.2
13. Interested/bored	51.0	22.8	28.1	67.6	43.4	24.2	−4.0
14. Withdrawn/sociable	55.5	66.0	10.6	30.6	51.4	20.4	+9.9
15. No sexual desire/aroused	30.6	40.4	9.8	14.1	24.7	10.6	+0.8
16. Impulsive/plan my actions	51.0	72.0	21.5	36.8	59.2	22.6	+1.1
17. Cheerful/depressed	63.0	27.6	35.4	79.8	52.8	27.0	−8.4
18. Trusting/suspicious	42.8	25.4	17.5	59.0	45.0	14.0	−3.5
19. No friends/many friends	57.2	66.7	9.5	40.8	51.6	10.8	+1.4
20. Chatty/quiet	57.1	39.1	18.0	68.4	41.6	26.8	+8.8
21. Angry/affectionate	48.1	64.9	16.7	37.9	48.5	10.6	−6.1
22. Full of hope/no hope	43.4	15.8	27.6	67.5	44.1	23.4	−4.2
23. Afraid/not afraid	30.7	47.9	17.3	28.1	34.6	6.5	−10.7
24. High/low self-regard	60.4	34.3	26.1	73.1	51.7	21.4	−4.7
25. Well-liked/disliked	40.2	27.1	13.1	51.4	43.2	8.2	−4.9
26. Capable/helpless	42.7	22.9	19.7	61.3	41.0	20.4	+0.6
27. Irritable/good-natured	48.1	67.4	19.3	43.7	46.2	2.5	−16.7
28. Want to get well/don't care	20.5	8.6	12.0	33.5	24.4	9.2	−1.8

The size and direction of the changes differed substantially. Improvement in mood is greater for some variables for patients with good recovery but for other variables, the converse obtains. With four measures, namely, drowsy (1), dreamy (10), withdrawn (14) and quiet (20), the higher baseline severity for the poor outcome patients is associated with more overall change than that shown for for the good improvers. Despite higher baseline anger (21) and depression (17) in the poor outcome group, they still show less change than good improvers.

For 16 of the twenty-eight measures shown, the net discrepancy change score between the two groups is less than 5 mm. In other words, the two groups show almost equal change on some sixteen measures despite their differing levels of disturbed mood at intake.

Feelings of hostility, anxiety, and irritability changed least for those patients showing a poor recovery. Loss of interest in sex never becomes fully restored for either group, perhaps because complaints of sexual dysfunction such as impotence or frigidity are rarely the focus of treatment in depressive states.

Only a minor difference is seen between groups on the capable–helpless dimension (26). Though poor improvers perceive themselves as the most helpless their final ratings place them at about the point where the good improvers were when they first entered hospital. On the 'want to get well' rating (28), the two groups differ only marginally in the overall degree of change shown.

Though in general depressed persons who are initially more severely ill are likely to change most, the present findings suggest that patients showing a poor recovery do not necessarily change less on *all* measures. By definition, of course, they remain worse overall by the treatment endpoint. A higher level of baseline psycho-pathology is thus not strictly equated with greater reduction of abnormal mood. On some measures on which the two groups are similarly impaired, the good outcome patients change most. On other measures (i.e., sadness, impulsivity, boredom, and muddled thinking) on which the poor recoverers register more initial impairment, only minor differences occur in the actual improvement shown by both groups. Thus, the relationship between such an event as therapeutic change and initial level of severity is complex.

Global severity of illness (not shown) also emerged as a factor distinguishing the good from the poor improver at intake ($t(1,46) = 2.27$, $p = 0.043$) and at discharge ($t(1,46) = 5.29$, $p < 0.001$). On a 6-point scale, the change for good improvers was

2.4, that for the poor improvers, 1.8. For total psychopathology, the good improvers had a discharge mean of 7.5 on the Hamilton Depression Scale, the poor improvers a mean of 18.4; the difference of 10 points was significant ($t = 5.48$, $df = 46$; $p < 0.001$).

MOOD-STATE VARIABILITY

Since mood patterns were studied over time their variability could be assessed and those feeling states which were fairly stable compared in detail with those which fluctuated rapidly. Of further interest was the question of whether some specific emotions might covary in synchrony or out of phase. This took into consideration not only the magnitude of change (mean deviation over days), but also the peaks and troughs in the profiles calculated separately for each patient using a longitudinal survey program (NEWLONG) developed by Dr. David Carter of the University of London Computing Centre.

The number of patients falling into the three categories of variability, high, moderate, and low, was determined (Table 10). Hostile–friendly was the most variable mood for approximately 60 per cent of the patients: high for 46, moderate for 21, and low for 3. Forty-two patients had a highly variable pattern in terms of how excited, sad, tense, or tired they felt. About 5 per cent of the plotted profiles for the total group reveal a basically invariant pattern.

Following the first 13 measures, the highest number of patients is to be found in the moderate variability column. Except for 9 measures, fewer than 10 patients are in the low variability column.

The two facets of anxiety appear to vary differently. Ratings of tension are highly variable for 42 patients but 31 patients show similar variability in terms of how afraid they feel. The fact that many patients show great variation in certain moods like anger, impulsivity, or suspicion suggests that persons might usefully be classified according to how they *covary* on these moods.

For most patients, certain moods were neither high nor low in variability but fluctuated moderately over time. Two measures in particular, clumsy and dreamy, followed a jagged course from depression to recovery with only one patient in the low variability column.

Two of the 28 mood dimensions, reduction of libido and motivation to improve, were characterized by low variability for 40 and 46

Table 10. *Mood-state variability over time*

Measures (code no. in Table 7)	High N	Moderate N	Low N	Mean Diff.*
1. Hostile/friendly (12)	46	21	3	8.07
2. Calm/excited (2)	42	24	4	13.05
3. Happy/sad (11)	42	26	4	32.67
4. Tense/relaxed (9)	42	23	5	22.71
5. Tired/energetic (6)	42	25	3	16.94
6. Mentally slow/quick-witted (8)	39	28	3	25.19
7. Strong/feeble (3)	38	27	5	27.72
8. Alert/drowsy (1)	38	25	7	25.67
9. Irritable/good-natured (27)	36	26	8	10.96
10. Angry/affectionate (21)	35	32	3	11.65
11. Trusting/suspicious (18)	35	31	4	15.25
12. Muzzy/clear-headed (4)	35	31	4	23.04
13. Cheerful/depressed (17)	34	34	2	33.43
14. Well co-ordinated/clumsy (5)	23	46	1	21.79
15. Attentive/dreamy (10)	27	42	1	22.41
16. Troubled/tranquil (7)	24	40	6	25.64
17. Chatty/quiet (20)	20	40	10	22.25
18. Interested/bored (13)	27	38	5	26.09
19. Withdrawn/sociable (14)	26	36	8	16.66
20. Afraid/not afraid (23)	31	36	3	12.11
21. Well-liked/disliked (25)	20	36	14	15.54
22. High/low self-regard (24)	16	36	18	24.36
23. No friends/many friends (19)	15	36	19	11.50
24. Capable/helpless (26)	25	34	11	26.14
25. Full of hope/no hope (22)	16	34	20	26.46
26. Impulsive/plan my actions (16)	28	31	11	23.29
27. Want to get well/don't care (28)	3	21	46	11.79
28. No sexual desire/aroused (15)	6	24	40	13.00

*Total change over treatment period.
The boxes link the highest number of patients in each category of variability for each measure.

patients respectively. It should be noted that many of the patients who demonstrated very little fluctuation, motivationally at least, were already at asymptote to begin with. On the other hand, several of the 40 patients with little fluctuation in their low baseline intensity of sexual excitation remained unimproved on this factor.

Mood-state variability and clinical improvement

An important distinction, but seldom made, is that between mood variability and actual mood change after recovery. An examination of the Mean Difference column in Table 10 confirms that the amount of mood change is not determined simply by whether most patients fit into any given variability category. The two measures of low mood (sad and depressed) changed most, but at least half of the sample had a highly variable pattern. Tension and excitability, two factors also with highly variable profiles, were only ranked as thirteenth and twenty-first in the overall amount of change. Feelings of boredom, with 38 patients falling into the moderate variability range, qualified as the sixth most responsive affect. Hostility, the most highly variable mood for 46 patients (some 60 per cent), failed to decrease significantly for the group as a whole. The plotted profiles show intrasubject variation to be quite substantial. Thus, it appears that mood fluctuation is not a good predictor of improvement.

SELF-RATINGS OF SLEEP

As disturbed sleep is a major defining feature of depression, the patients' self-monitoring of their sleep patterns during recovery from depression is of practical interest. The profiles over 50 days show that onset of sleep was quicker for about 80 per cent of the total group ($p < 0.01$). More change occurred during the first 10 days after admission to hospital than during the subsequent 40 days. Self-rated quality of sleep improved slightly up to the fourth week, after which a slight decline set in. Thus it appears that this aspect of sleep is not consistently improved by tricyclic antidepressant medication.

A third measure, feeling on wakening, rose from sleepy (baseline mean = 27 mm) to a moderate alertness (discharge mean = 75 mm). The major shift took place during the third week after admission ($p < 0.001$) with no further remission.

On recovery, self-rated morning mood improved remarkably, as many patients no longer felt sad or hopeless after awakening. Early morning awakening occurred very infrequently for most patients (i.e., twice monthly) but still diminished markedly over time ($p < 0.001$).

Patients fall asleep more quickly but still awaken earlier than usual 'once in a while' (about twice a month). Observer ratings in the Hamilton Rating Scale confirm the significant reduction in initial insomnia by the third week of in-patient care (see Fig. 1).

Relationship between self-ratings and Hamilton ratings

Correlations between the self-ratings and Hamilton ratings were generally significant (Table 11). Disturbed self-regard correlates with four of the selected Hamilton ratings shown. Observer and patients' ratings of sadness do not correlate strongly, psychic anxiety showing a higher correlation with patients' sadness.

Table 11. *Within-patient correlations between Hamilton Depression scores and patient self-ratings*

| Hamilton ratings | Patient ratings (Prime symptoms) | | | | |
	Self-image	Sadness	Feebleness	Impulsivity	Fear
Depressed mood	0.27	0.39	0.36	–	0.37
Suicidal intent	0.43	0.43	0.55	−0.50	0.27
Psychic anxiety	0.31	0.48	0.36	−0.48	0.53
Initial insomnia	–	0.34	0.30	−0.26	–
Loss of libido	–	0.32	–	–	–
Depersonalization	–	0.30	0.23	−0.39	–
Inability to work	0.31	0.43	0.30	–	0.34
Loss of insight	–	0.38	–	–	–

$r > 0.26, p < 0.05$.
$r > 0.32, p < 0.01$
$r > 0.42, p < 0.001$.
Dashes indicate no significant correlation.

The tendency to act impulsively is negatively correlated with four of the eight Hamilton ratings, but not with depressed mood. Fear correlates well with psychic anxiety.

Suicidal intent and psychic anxiety are correlated across all five prime patient-rated symptoms, whereas loss of libido relates only to sadness and loss of insight only to sad affect.

PREDICTORS OF CLINICAL STATUS AT DISCHARGE

The pre-treatment scores of the demographic, mood, psychomotor, and cognitive measures were analysed to determine which measures were predictive of good as compared with poor psychiatric outcome.

Table 12. *Clinical, mood, and performance factors predictive of good and poor outcome (as defined by post-treatment HRSD scores at discharge)*

Measure	Good improvers (N = 23)	Poor improvers (N = 25)	P (t-test)
Clinical			
1. Pre-HRSD score (total)	27.2	35.5	0.001
2. Length of stay (weeks)	8.7	12.2	0.005
3. Previous admissions (number)	0.7	1.8	0.010
4. Age (years)	37.7	43.0	–
5. Age of onset (years)	33.7	39.1	–
6. Episode duration (weeks)	19.7	21.5	–
7. Previous episodes (number)	1.6	2.6	0.041
Mood			
1. Muzzy/clear-headed	59.7	34.1	0.001
2. Attentive/dreamy	42.0	60.2	0.021
3. Hostile/friendly	55.7	53.2	–
4. Trusting/suspicious	42.8	59.0	0.037
5. Mentally slow/quick-witted	49.3	33.7	0.028
6. Cheerful/depressed	63.0	79.8	0.015
7. No sexual desire/aroused	30.6	14.1	0.003
8. Well co-ordinated/clumsy	41.5	55.4	–
9. Helpless/capable	42.7	61.3	0.014
10. Tense/relaxed	22.3	17.1	–
11. Afraid/not afraid	30.7	28.1	–
12. Troubled/tranquil	21.2	18.3	–
13. Withdrawn/sociable	55.5	30.9	0.002
14. Chatty/quiet	57.1	68.4	–
15. Full of hope/no hope	43.4	67.5	0.008
16. Impulsive/plan my actions	51.0	36.8	0.075
17. Happy/sad	59.0	78.2	0.017
18. Strong/feeble	49.8	66.4	0.030
19. Tired/energetic	40.5	27.5	0.036
20. High/low self-regard	60.4	73.1	0.048
Psychomotor			
1. Tapping rate	99.6	91.8	–
2. Symbol Copying Test	79.7	77.9	–
3. Digit Symbol Substitution Test	34.3	35.0	–
4. Gibson Spiral Maze (time)	93.0	100.4	–
5. Gibson Spiral Maze (errors)	2.3	3.3	–
Cognitive			
1. Paired-Associates (easy)	4.9	4.9	–
2. Paired-Associates (hard)	0.7	0.8	–
3. Logical memory (paragraph 1)	8.3	7.2	–
4. Logical memory (paragraph 2)	6.5	5.9	–

All patients were split into the highest, medium, and lowest scoring thirds according to their rank-order on the Hamilton Rating Scale for Depression (HRSD) at discharge. Since time spent in hospital differed from patient to patient, the final HRSD was completed at different times.

Measures predictive of treatment outcome (good outcome, $N = 23$; poor outcome $N = 25$; medium outcome excluded $N = 22$), were then subjected to separate univariate t-tests (Table 12).

Two of the 15 clinical and life history measures could significantly distinguish the good from the poor responder; they were low pre-Hamilton scores and shorter duration of stay.

Of the 28 mood measures, 13 contributed significantly to inter-group discrimination. Muddled thinking (1), inattention (2), and suspicion (4) are examples of such measures. Depressed mood (6) and reduced sex drive (7) also differ between good and poor improvers.

The measure of helplessness (9) is also significant, that is, subjects who feel less helpless have a better outcome. They are also more hopeful (15), slightly more sociable (13), can think more clearly (5), and are less withdrawn (13). The two outcome groups did not differ in their level of physical tension (10), anxiety (11), or troubled affect (12).

Hopelessness (15) and lowered self-regard (20) are two measures on which poor recoverers rated themselves more highly than good recoverers on the first testing. Though the pessimistic outlook on life and negative self-concept of good and poor improvers alike declines significantly over time, the two outcome groups continue to remain differentiated on these two indices at discharge.

Nevertheless, the ratings on discharge of the poor responders do not imply a positive self-view. Low self-regard, indicative of the depressive cognitive style, is not reversed in the final self-estimates of the poor improvers. By contrast, the end-point for good improvers suggests they now feel more self-assured and confident.

No differences were detected with respect to psychomotor or cognitive functions.

SEX DIFFERENCES

Table 13 presents the t-test analyses of the mood, perceptual-motor and personal-life history measures for 28 male and 42 female

Table 13. *Sex differences in initial mood, psychomotor, and clinical rating scores for 28 male and 42 female depressives*

Variable	Males Mean SD	Females Mean SD	t-diff. (df = 1,68)	p
Moods				
Muzzy/clear-headed	35.3 ± 19.8	50.3 ± 31.4	−2.12	0.04
Hostile/friendly	43.6 ± 21.8	61.7 ± 22.4	−2.85	0.007
Chatty/quiet	73.2 ± 24.0	58.5 ± 34.0	1.82	0.07
Full of hope/no hope	68.0 ± 24.2	50.7 ± 25.6	2.07	0.04
Want to get well/don't care	42.4 ± 12.4	16.7 ± 10.7	3.08	0.004
Psychomotor/cognitive				
Gibson Spiral Maze (errors)	2.1 ± 1.6	3.3 ± 2.6	−2.15	0.04
Logical memory (paragraph 2)	7.1 ± 2.7	5.4 ± 2.8	2.16	0.04
Hamilton rating scale for depression				
Suicidal ideation	2.8 ± 1.1	1.8 ± 1.2	3.06	0.004
Agitation	1.4 ± 0.8	1.0 ± 0.5	2.01	0.05
Demographic factors				
Employed (yes–no)	0.7 ± 0.5	0.3 ± 0.2	2.55	0.015

depressives at intake. Only 10 of the 74 differences reached significance. Males appear to view themselves as less clear-headed, more hostile, and less talkative than females. Females had more positive ratings for desired improvement, suggesting that they were more motivated than males and were also more hopeful.

By and large, females remain more highly motivated throughout. However, by the treatment end-point, the difference is just outside usual significance levels (males $\chi = 24.0$, females $\chi = 11.5$, $t(1,68) = 1.93$, $p = 0.066$). As recovery proceeds, males increase in their ratings of hope and desire to be well again. Two additional sex differences became evident during the final testing period: males feel less alert than do females ($t = 2.11$, $df = 1,68$, $p = 0.041$), while females feel stronger than do males ($t = 2.11$, $df = 1,68$, $p = 0.041$).

On the whole, the self-report data fail to support the notion of sex differences in perceptions of stress-coping responses or intensity of affective symptoms. No sex differences emerged for troubled mood, bodily tension, sadness, anxiety, or lowered self-esteem, all major aspects of depressive illness.

Given the high intra-individual variability of patients on cognitive and perceptual-motor tasks, it is not surprising that few sex differences occurred. Females made more errors on the Gibson Spiral Maze but no sex differences were found for tapping rate, SCT, DSST, time taken to complete the maze tracing or the Paired-Associate learning task, irrespective of item-pair difficulty level. Females outperformed males on the second paragraph of the Logical Memory task.

On the HRSD males had a significantly higher 'suicidal intent' score than females. Agitation also distinguished the two sexes, but only just ($p < 0.05$). Staff impressions of male patients support the finding that they are more readily disposed to anger or hostility. Even after full or partial remission of their depressive episode, the two sexes are largely the same on all the Hamilton indices, except for one symptomatic complaint: middle of the night insomnia ($t(1,68) = 2.66$; $p = 0.01$).

5. Discussion

This chapter attempts to collate the various findings and to relate them to previous work. The results will be discussed in relation to each of the questions formulated earlier.

SEQUENCING OF MOOD PATTERNS

The sequencing of the patients' predominant moods from depressed state to partial or full recovery is complex. Thus, owing to lower initial levels, feelings of helplessness and hopelessness were reversed before depressed mood, as predicted by Beck (1974, 1976) and co-workers (Beck et al., 1979).

Depressed mood improved more than low self-esteem, hopelessness, and feelings of helplessness, but not by much. And yet, many patients continued to feel more sad than helpless or hopeless at the treatment end-point.

The level of motivation of most patients remained high and varied little during treatment, suggesting that many patients were already at, or near, a plateau. This is counter to the claim by Seligman (1975, 1978) that feelings of helplessness produced motivational deficits. Patients entered hospital reasonably well motivated and aspired to become well again despite their perceived degree of helplessness.

Expectancy change ratings, in success-failure manipulation studies, have come under criticism (Payne, 1980) as confounded (Rizley, 1978) and as invalid (Blaney, 1977; Abramson et al., 1978). Some therorists have argued that high motivation may facilitate recovery from depression (Mendels, 1970; Beck et al., 1974; Becker, 1974). However, our results suggest that such motivation did not help patients reduce feelings of anxiety, anger, irritability, or hostility. Many patients remained continuously unwell despite a strong desire to recover. The validity of self-assessments of motivation are very questionable, since some patients had little 'real' interest in changing their behaviour.

Two aspects of depression, anxiety and negative self-opinion, did not recover in parallel as some patients reported an enhanced self-concept despite some persistent mental anxiety. Prior to treatment and at discharge, anxiety and self-concept were negatively correlated. This supports the hypothesis that a person can be anxious without loss of self-esteem (Spielberger, 1972). The fact that somatic and emotional-cognitive components of anxiety are highly interrelated (Tyrer, 1976; Klerman, 1977) is supported by our results. Over time the various aspects of anxiety covaried but never disappeared completely. This confirms Tyrer's (1976) observation that 'changes in subjective anxiety are much more gradual and show less fluctuation than mean bodily symptom ratings' (p. 56).

A clear-cut pattern emerged of a concordant relationship between feelings of sadness and perceived helplessness: the more capable patients feel, the happier they become. Whether feelings of helplessness were a consequence or an antecedent condition of depression, moderate correlations of the order of 0.5 were found between these two concepts at admission. This relationship became stronger as existing feelings of helplessness and sad affect resolved.

These data accord with literature on the learned helplessness model of depression. Thus, Raps and his co-workers (1980) demonstrated in a psychiatric population that a mood-elation procedure could reverse the learned helplessness effect and depressive affect caused by helplessness training, though the effects were short-lived.

An unexpected finding involved hostility. Many depressed patients when they improved clinically, still felt hostile towards the world. Also the patients tended to remain irritable and angry. Anger and irritability, like hostility, followed a variable course, not synchronous over time, and failed to improve significantly within 4 to 6 weeks when other symptoms had largely subsided. Further similar evidence is provided by Perris and co-workers (1979) who found no lessening of hostility or aggression in 30 hospitalized depressives from admission to discharge. Klerman and Gershon (1970) and Friedman (1970) also report that the redirection of hostility outward was not essential to recovery from depression.

In conclusion, the intricacies of mood sequences from depression to recovery ranged all the way from close correspondence, for example, rising self-esteem accompanied by a drop in the level of feelings of boredom, sadness, and hopelessness to almost complete dissociation of the variables.

TEMPORAL RELATIONSHIP OF MOODS, SYMPTOMS, AND PERFORMANCE TASKS

Changes in mood, symptoms, and perceptual-motor functions did not proceed hand in hand in accordance with theoretical predictions: some measures did not change, other measures lessened rapidly and markedly, while still others were delayed. Thus, depressive illness is characterized by a fluctuating, waxing and waning clinical course.

Over the initial 5-week period, core features of patients' depressed state, such as feelings of hopelessness, helplessness, boredom and low sense of self-worth improved at about the same rate as depressed mood. This early mood lifting varied widely from patient to patient. Concurrent feelings of hostility, anxiety, or anger took longer to remit. On the anxiety component, many worries persisted, apparently unaffected by tricyclic medication or supportive counselling. Similar desynchrony occurs with the behavioural, emotional and physiological indices of fear (Lang, 1977; Rachman, 1978), subtypes of hostility (Friedman, 1970; Pilowsky & Spence, 1975) and components of guilt (Shapiro, 1979; Mosher, 1979), and may also apply to other mood states associated with 'success' or 'failure' experiences.

Personal worth (rated on the Symptom Q-Sort) improved slightly overall. Some patients still found difficulty admitting that they had any favourable personal characteristics. On the other hand, according to their self-reports on the visual analogue scales (which do not assess frequency), their degree of low personal worth significantly improved from point of intake to day 35. Note, however, that the Symptom Q-Sort format is based on *frequency of occurrence*, the linear analogue scales on *intensity of experience*. Hence changes may vary from scale to scale. Moreover, the extent to which different scale formats may influence responses is unclear. The patients may adopt a more positive self-view in terms of the intensity of feeling as they recover, but it may be some time before the frequency of experience alters. This underlines the need for separate measures of the frequency, intensity, and duration of feelings of self-reported depression.

Slowed psychomotor activity was reversed over the first two weeks after admission, as were other accompanying bodily features of the depressive state. After the fourth week, further improvement was negligible. Psychomotor quickening followed a monotonic, negatively accelerating curve, much like learning curves and in agreement with many earlier findings (Hall & Stride, 1954; Fisher, 1949; Callagan, 1952; Mayo, 1966, 1967; Simpson *et al.*, 1976; Cecchini *et al.*, 1978; Heshe *et al.*, 1978; Rapp, 1978; Tsutsui *et al.*, 1979). However, in other studies, depressives showed either only minor motor retardation, or disruptions of motor activity that lessened clinical improvement. Some of these findings comprised only test-retest data for a single psychomotor task, the DSST, or simple reaction time (RT) and, in other studies, may have been confounded by the recent application of ECT.

As patients were prescribed different types and dosage levels of anxiolytic and antidepressant drugs, it was impracticable to study specific drug effects. Another inherent difficulty was whether impairment was due to the lowered ability of patients in discriminating or recognizing stimuli (input processes), to actual motor slowing (output processes), to impaired short-term memory, or to general slowing of cognitive processes.

Mean performance for Logical Memory and Paired-Associate Learning peaked around the fifth week. Patients were only minimally impaired in their ability to learn easy word-pairs. Thus, the paired easy associate test was not sensitive enough to detect the type of cognitive slowing found in moderate-to-severe depression. However, with some learning tasks difficulty is experienced by depressives in encoding and retrieving easy or difficult word-pair associations. Besides Friedman (1964), several researchers have found impairment of such learning to be related to depression (Cronholm & Ottosson, 1961; Velten, 1968; Sternberg & Jarvik, 1976). Logical memory, by contrast, improved markedly.

As already mentioned, the possibility of some 'practice effects' cannot be excluded. Learning may have enhanced motor or memory performance on some of these tasks despite the use of parallel test forms. However, the tasks used rely heavily on the motor component (for example, steadiness, eye-hand co-ordination, and reaction time) are fairly uncontaminated by learning.

GLOBAL SEVERITY RATINGS

At intake the strongest association with severity of depression was to anxiety, followed by bodily tension and sadness (range: $r = 0.39$ to 0.46). On the final assessment, twice as many significant correlations had arisen between observer-rated severity and the patient's mood descriptions. The more important of these were happy mood, renewed interest, motivation to become well, and a hopeful attitude.

The evidence cited by Miller (1975) favouring the adverse impact on psychomotor functioning of severity of illness is based mostly on between-group contrast of normal and pathological individuals in whom differences in severity and motor retardation are already self-evident. This analogy may not necessarily apply to a within-group comparison of depressives only. In our study, good and poor improvers did not differ in their psychomotor tempo. The motor retardation of some patients may not be due to a common factor such as 'poor motivation', as suggested by Miller (1975), since the initial self-reports suggest that the patients, even the eventual poor recoverers, wanted to co-operate and get well.

It is well known that severity of depression is closely aligned to a host of somatic features which accompany the depressive state (Schwab *et al.*, 1965; Mendels & Cochrane, 1968; Katz, 1971; Beck, 1976). Some depressives still see themselves as continously unwell, which is consistent with the finding that between 15 and 30 per cent of depressed individuals do not get better and may relapse (Toone & Ron, 1977).

INFLUENCES OF MOOD ON COGNITIVE PROCESSES

Patients evidently construed their subjectively felt anxiety and depression as more intense and more debilitating than their devalued self-concept. While all three – anxiety, sadness and low self-regard – have been regarded as core features of the depressive state (Bibring, 1953; Mendels, 1970; Anthony & Benedek, 1975), the primacy of any one has not been clearly established. Emotional intensity influences memory and, according to Bower (1981), influences such cognitive processes as free associations, social perceptions, imaginative fantasies, and snap judgements about others' personalities.

In trying to account for the correlations between sadness, anxiety, and self-concept, the pattern of symptom remission cannot elucidate whether cognition causally determines affect (Beck, 1970, 1976) or, as Lewinsohn (1974) contends, 'the cognitive aspects of depression are just the secondary elaboration of feelings of dysphoria' (p. 169). Most likely, sadness, anxiety, and low self-concept share some common causes, identification of which is important. Since the disturbances are by definition not identifiable in terms of the measures used in the present study one can only speculate on the causal influence of one on the other.

Though depressed mood and low self-worth differed in intensity both changed early during treatment and followed a synchronous pattern to confirm Beck's (1974, 1976) view of their close association. Though correlated over time, it cannot be concluded that a negative self-view precedes depression (Beck, 1967). Brandon (1973) suggests that only a change in self-concept will alleviate the depressed mood state. In the present study, both improved synchronously to suggest some dependent relationship. In general, the precise interaction between self-esteem and depressed mood remains to be established, despite much theoretical speculation.

The close relationship between hopelessness and clinical depression which emerged has previously been documented (Bibring,1953; Beck *et al.*, 1974; Brandon, 1973). Feelings of hopelessness were related as less intense than anxiety or sadness, were less variable, and, unlike anxiety, remitted relatively faster. Downward shifts in the more cognitively-oriented measures like feelings of hopelessness and helplessness did not precede reductions in the intensity of depressed mood. They all, evidently, diminished concurrently.

One of the most robust findings in the literature on the depressive syndrome is that hopelessness is a prominent feature of the disorder (Beck *et al.*, 1974, 1975; Kovacs & Beck, 1978; Wetzel *et al.*, 1980). Hopelessness correlated positively with depressed mood, but not global severity, at intake, to support Beck's hypothesis. Another crucial factor, helplessness, a central component of the depressive attributional style (Seligman, 1975, 1978; Miller & Seligman, 1975; Abramson *et al.*, 1978, Telner & Singhal, 1984), also correlated with depressed mood (but not overall severity) before and after treatment.

Thus, global severity lacks validity when compared with the patients' self- reports of certain moods and cognitions commonly linked to clinical depression. In this context, observer ratings of severity of illness may have limited validity and they should be viewed with caution.

The question of whether feeling precedes thinking as proposed by Zajonc (1980) or whether thinking determines a specific emotion

(Beck, 1971, 1976) is still controversial (Rachman, 1981). However, evidence is accruing that cognitive manipulations can induce mood and behaviour changes in normal and depressed subjects (Blaney, 1977; Kovacs & Beck, 1978).

Another important finding relates to the discrepancy between the patients' initial despair about future prospects and their desire for recovery and a better life style. One possible, but not entirely satisfactory, explanation is that the admission of helplessness and hopelessness may be based on their patients having felt this way all along. In contrast, their expectations of 'getting well' may be based on their belief that in hospital they will now get well. Those depressives with multiple episodes who have recovered in the past will feel optimistic about the outcome of their present admission. If so, many patients may perceive their depression as temporary.

PREDICTORS OF PSYCHIATRIC OUTCOME

Patients having a good outcome were less seriously ill on admission than those with poor outcome. Severity of illness was the single best discriminator between neurotic and psychotic depression (Ni Bhlor-chain *et al.*, 1979) and a good predictor of improvement among four groups of depressives (Paykel *et al.*, 1973a).

Conversely pre-treatment severity and clinical outcome were unrelated in out-patient depressives (Young *et al.*, 1976). However, global severity has been differently defined across studies, sometimes on one scale only and at other times in terms of the total Hamilton, Beck, or Zung Depression rating scales. In comparing one study to another, such distinctions are often overlooked.

A prominent feature in the poor improvers was their more intense feelings of helplessness and hopelessness. With treatment, feelings of helplessness and hopelessness were significantly improved and, unexpectedly, actually attained a more satisfactory level when compared to the patients' residual depression. Following recovery, patients' self-esteem was less than their residual sadness, implying that the treatment did not particularly enhance the low self-concept of patients. This underlines the need to utilize more specific forms of affect or cognitive modification to alter certain treatment-resistant aspects like mental anxiety or diminished self-esteem (Rachman, 1981).

Patients with the most or least favourable outcome remained

indistinguishable in terms of how tense, impulsive, hostile, angry, anxious, disliked, or unmotivated they felt at admission. Other analyses suggested that good and poor improvers were the same in their frequency of suicidal thinking, sex, marital and employment status, and positive family history of psychiatric disorder. The fact that none of these indices was a useful predicator of good or poor recovery is rather unexpected.

The findings that poor and good recoverers have similar subjective complaints has several implications. Firstly, the 'mixed' clinical picture makes diagnostic discrimination between anxiety and depressive states or other hypothesized subtypes of depression more difficult (Downing & Rickels, 1974; Prusoff & Klerman, 1974), particularly in cases where diagnostic impressions change with successive hospital admissions. Secondly, given the controversy about whether clinical depression is basically a mood/affective disorder (Hamilton, 1974; Spitzer *et al.*, 1977; Klerman, 1977) or a thought disorder (Beck, 1976), it remains to be established whether patients who recover partially or fully can be more reliably distinguished on the basis of their emotions or cognitions.

Rather unexpectedly again, the two outcome groups could not be separated on the basis of their perceptual-motor or cognitive functioning. Kerr and co-workers (1974) also found that retarded motor activity did not predict psychiatric outcome. For Paykel and co-workers (1973a), a measure of retardation just fell short of qualifying as a predictor of mood change. On the other hand, Beck and co-workers (1962) found a statistically significant relationship between digit-symbol performance and severity of self-rated depression. Thus, given these discrepant findings, the relationship between slowed psychomotor funtioning, severity of illness, and clinical outcome is unclear.

DURATION OF PRESENT DEPRESSIVE EPISODE

Most patients left hospital within three months with partial to full symptom remission. Only 7 of 70 patients failed to satisfy the psychiatric discharge criteria (cf. Feighner *et al.*, 1972; Spitzer *et al.*, 1978) and stayed in hospital more than 90 days. This accords with data of Kolakowska (1975) indicating that 26 of 70 patients remitted only partially although they were all discharged within one to three months. A longer period of hospitalization is, of course, not uncommon. Toone & Ron (1977) report that length of stay exceeded three months in 18 of 30 depressives. In our study, only two patients relapsed briefly: both were re-admitted to hospital and discharged within six weeks.

SEVERITY AND MOOD CHANGE

One problem in combining patients into any arbitrarily defined category, such as level of severity or current emotional intensity, is that they do not change consistently across the various moods. Theoretically, at least, a higher level of initial psychopathology should result in greater decrease in abnormal mood. Among others, Paykel and co-workers (1973a) found that the more seriously ill the patient, the greater the symptomatic relief reported by the patient. However, for some emotions, for example, fear or tiredness, such a relationship did not hold, though it did for others, for example, low self-worth, sadness, and hopelessness.

Though a higher intensity of any felt emotion may be prognostic of a significant improvement, the degree of change relative to initial level is a separate issue. To summarize, our findings do not imply that the most elevated moods necessarily change most, only that proportionately more of the severely ill patients register a significant improvement upon discharge. When the patient was relieved of his major symptoms, the remaining, less acute symptoms were less disturbing. Many classic signs of depression were still quite resistant to the type of psychiatric care in the two teaching hospitals in the study.

MOOD-STATE VARIABILITY

Specific emotional states may be highly variable for one patient and stable for another. Considering the findings for anxious, hostile, or depressed mood, the individual scatterplots showed about equal numbers of patients with moderately or extremely variable patterns. Hence, no one mood dimension can be designated highly variable nor stable for all patients. Variability of any given mood over time in individual patients is often obscured by the mood variability for the group as a whole.

Differences between our patients were marked. Presumably the experience and interpretation of distinct emotional states varies according to the person's individual threshold, dominant character traits, the way people draw inferences from interpersonal events, and other selective biases. Depending, too, on frustration tolerance, some emotions are construed as quite distressful, others as only mildly upsetting. Few graphic data are available to illustrate the mood swings in depression although Lewis (1936) was among the first to examine the covariation between moods and symptoms in his classic study of 61 Maudsley depressives.

MOOD-STATE VARIABILITY AND CLINICAL IMPROVEMENT

An important question concerns mood variability and clinical improvement. Our data suggest an imperfect relationship between the two. Feelings like hostility, anger, or irritability which are extremely variable for up to half of all patients, showed no greater change than did less variable moods. Yet extreme variability is for most patients indicative of a large reduction in feelings of drowsiness, weakness, sadness, and mental sluggishness.

Mendels (1970) reported that great variability of mood occurs during patients' very depressed periods. As depression lifts, patients no longer oscillate between cheerfulness and depression, but few of the moods we studied exhibited a truly stable or invariant pattern as patients recovered.

In conclusion, differences between patients were striking. As Blackburn & Bonham (1980) observed, 'each patient appears to have his own particular relationship where intensity and relationship between moods vary'. Mood-state variability is thus differentially related to reductions in the intensity of a felt emotion. Neither extreme nor moderate variability of mood is linked to the degree of improvement.

ANXIETY AND DEPRESSION

Next, we shall consider the relationship between anxiety and depression. The precise nosological relations between anxiety and depression still remain unclear (Downing & Rickels, 1974). During the first three weeks in hospital, when patients were most ill, anxious and depressed mood covaried. Thereafter this concordant relationship broke down: depressive feelings declined most, followed by a moderate decrease in the patients' level of somatic tension, though various subjective fears remained static. These residual signs of pathological anxiety persisted.

Much the same pattern emerged on the Symptom Q-Sort. The somatic components of anxiety recovered more rapidly than the concomitant worrisome thought and feelings. The most highly-rated symptom, 'I worry a lot' had the slowest and most incomplete remission. Severe anxiety of long duration appears to respond poorly to a non-specific treatment approach.

Since the initial level of bodily tension was more elevated than depressed or anxious mood for the group, one might expect more change to occur on that factor. However, somatic tension changed less than feelings of depression but more than subjective anxiety. This is consistent with earlier findings (Simpson *et al.*, 1976; Vaisanen *et al.*, 1978) indicating that depressives had lower levels of somatic than of psychic anxiety after one month of antidepressant therapy.

The current data support previous findings with depressed individuals, all showing partial rather than full remission of clinical anxiety (Prusoff *et al.*, 1976; Young *et al.*, 1976; Simpson *et al.*, 1976). In three studies (Young *et al.*, 1976; Simpson *et al.*, 1976; Vaisanen *et al.*, 1978) depressed mood decreased more than mental anxiety, irrespective of tricyclic drug or dosage level given. Why mental anxiety remits slowly is still unknown.

STABILITY OF MOOD, MEMORY, AND PAIRED-ASSOCIATE LEARNING

For practical reasons, memory and learning were measured weekly, moods every other day. Even after allowing for this, the profiles for most moods reveal more peaks and troughs than do those of the patients' psychomotor or cognitive performance. Moreover, the curvilinear recovery curves of the patients' perceptual-motor and cognitive impairment showed no deterioration. In contrast, the plotted mood profiles showed clear progress, slipped back, then spurted ahead before becoming normal. Though patients complained vociferously of their cognitive loss, they varied little in their overall performance. Using regression slope as an index of change, the reversal of cognitive deficits was faster than that of certain feelings (for example anxiety, anger, or hostility) and noticeably slower than others (for example, boredom, sadness, or hopelessness). Depression, memory recall, and word-pair learning substantially improved, though only depressed mood varied much. As Miller (1975) concluded in his review of psychological deficits in depression, various observed deficits in verbal learning and memory occur in depressed patients. The aetiology of these may lie in the 'cognitive interference', 'reduced motivation' or state of 'learned helplessness' experienced by depressed individuals. Our patients were still motivated to recover and were not extremely helpless, judging by their self-reports. However, they did report much 'cognitive interference' in the form of distracting thoughts, worries, and poor self-esteem; these competed for the depressed individual's attention and disrupted his performance on many different tasks.

Costello (1978) has argued cogently that depressives may not necessarily be deficient in their verbal learning ability. This is partly borne out by impaired memory recall despite the patients' normal ability to learn easy word-pairs. Lang & Frith (1981) have demonstrated a 'reminscence effect' on a pursuit learning task: a group of depressives did not outperform control subjects but could integrate and remember predictable target movements. Depressives experience difficulty in actually executing the required motor movements and this factor largely accounts for their poorer performance. Though some evidence supports all of Miller's (1975) three basic hypotheses concerning psychological deficits in depression, the issue of aetiology is far from being resolved and calls for studies to test these theories.

GENERAL CONCLUSIONS

One major question unanswered by this research is the extent to which certain characteristics of the depressive state, like excessive self-blame, low personal worth, hopelessness, clinical anxiety, and melancholy mood, are causally related. At present, neither cognitive nor affective models of depression address themselves to the possible aetiology of unipolar or bipolar depression. As Weissman & Paykel (1974) have noted, the relationships between mood and cognition remain indirect, inferential, and problematic. The most heuristic hypothesis for future study is that depressed mood and negative cognitions share some common causal paths. It would be interesting to explore the extent to which these variables can be manipulated, to determine possible causal relations between them and thus perhaps to manipulate depression itself.

Mood as well as physical symptoms and negative thought patterns change at different rates and in different directions. At times one or more of the systems may be partly discordant with the other. Thus, during therapy the investigator may encounter differences between motor, physiological, and verbal self-report indices of emotions and at least three different types of measure are required in any valid assessment of therapeutic outcome. Theoretically, at least, the treatment technique should match the primarily disturbed component. Future investigation with depressed individuals could show whether psychotherapy, pharmacology, cognitive behaviour therapy, or 'spontaneous remission' produce a greater degree of concordance among measures in different systems.

The fact that general levels of hostility, anger, guilt, anxious mood, and specific cognitive distortions remit relatively slowly has important general implications. These troublesome factors will remain largely unaffected by general treatment programmes, so that more specific techniques (for example, self-control strategies, affective insight therapy, or adopting a 'neutral' attitude toward a thought or feeling) are most effective for curtailing the intensity, frequency, or duration of some disruptive thought or affective reaction.

The topic of cognitive functioning in the depressive disorders is a complex and fascinating one, from both its clinical and theoretical aspects. Helping patients to reappraise the initial situation somewhat more rationally and to react in more appropriate ways serves to create a heightened sense of self-efficacy. However, in the present study, certain patients exhibited a definite 'cognitive lag'. During remission, some depressive patients may still be making negative causal attributions (for example, I'm still helpless or unworthy) despite their early lifting of mood. Further explorations might focus on the cognitive style and causal attributions made by persons illustrating such a pattern, to assess if and how differences in these functions help to account for the patients' residual psychopathology.

It is important to determine whether the patient's level of motivation remains constant, as changes in this may produce changes in behaviour which are unrelated to the effects of therapy. In the current investigation, desire for improvement altered little over time. Thus, there is a need to distinguish between intellectually and emotionally-based expectancies. Efforts might be directed toward isolating the separate effects of the various expectancies held by investigators and patients.

During testing, a discrepancy arose between the patients' subjective working memory and clinical tests of memory functioning. Some patients still complained of memory loss, even though their performance on laboratory tests of memory steadily improved. From a clinical and theoretical perspective, laboratory tasks need to reflect more accurately the real-life memory deficits that are complained of by individual patients. An expanded study might address the issue of remedial programming for situation-specific memory deficiencies.

Moderate to severe anxiety of long duration seems integral to the depression-prone individual, irrespective of eventual therapeutic outcome. Psychological anxiety in particular, whether 'free-floating' or linked to a specific stressor, was mainly unaffected by drug therapy or any spontaneous remission which might have occurred. A therapeutic approach to excessive anxiety might well focus on raising the individual's expectancy of goal attainment, or possibly decreasing the significance of overvalued goals. Patients with much residual ('anticipatory') fear might be treated behaviourally.

One unexpected finding was the similarity in perceptual-motor activity, memory retrieval, and verbal learning in patients with a good or poor clinical recovery. It may be more useful to predict differential response to treatment by means of life-history and mood measures. The patient's affective reactions emerged as the most important predictor of improved or unimproved clinical status.

It is apparent that the symptom profile patterns of depressed patients are complex. Shifts in motor, cognitive, or emotional responses did not proceed hand in hand according to a simple theoretical paradigm. Patients, evidently, start at different severity levels and improve at different rates. What this suggests, with certain provisos, is that the most pathological mood or negative thinking patterns do not change by some optimal amount for *all* patients simply because of a greater margin for improvement.

Why this is so is largely a matter for speculation. The data suggest a time lag between changes in depressive affect and those in other variables. If so, it is important to examine the sequencing of multiple mood patterns from illness to recovery. A better understanding of the interrelationships of these variables is also important for issues in therapy outcome research. Future studies might seek to establish whether the same pattern of affective or cognitive lags uncovered by the current research are also characteristic of groups of patients with other mental disorders.

6. Summary

A longitudinal study of 70 depressed patients established differential rates of recovery of the various components of depression over the first few weeks of hospitalization. Clinical progress was monitored by self-and observer-ratings of mood, a symptom Q-sort, and tests of psychomotor and cognitive functioning.

Deficits in mood and cognition were substantially reduced after patients had spent five weeks in hospital. Marked differences emerged in the *severity* and *rate* of response of various components of the depressive illness. Sad affect, lack of interest, hopelessness, helplessness, suicidal thinking, and somatic dysfunction rapidly recovered. An intermediate rate was observed for low self-esteem, sleep disturbances, cognitive slowing, impulsivity, emtional blunting, self-criticism, anhedonia, and subjective memory complaints. Specific features like guilt, intropunitive anger, acquiescence, low expectancies, indecision, suspicion, hostility, diminished libido, and anxiety remitted slowly. After five weeks, performance on psychomotor, immediate memory, and paired-associate learning tasks reached a plateau.

Good and poor improvers differed with respect to their initial Hamilton Depression scores and several mood elements, but not by an index of perceptual-motor functioning.

The data are, in general, consistent with the 'learned helplessness' and 'cognitive' models of human depression, since patients feel more hopeful, more worthy, and less helpless as their depression lifts. However, shifts in the intensity and frequency of the more cognitively-mediated and mood dimensions of depression do not necessarily precede, or follow, but are *parallel* to one other. Therefore, the findings suggest a reciprocal relationship between cognition and depression without determining cause or effect.

References

Abou-Saleh, M. T. & Coppen, A. (1983). Classification of depression and response to antidepressive therapies. *Brit. J. Psychiat.*, **143**, 601–3.

Abramson, L. Y., Seligman, M. E. P. & Teasdale, J. D. (1978). Learned helplessness in humans: critique and reformulation. *J. Abn. Psychol.*, **87**, 49–74.

Aitken, R. C. B. (1969). Measurement of feelings using visual analogue scales. *Proc. Soc. Med.*, **62**, 989–93.

—— & Zealley, A. K. (1970). The measurement of moods. *Brit. J. Hosp. Med.*, **4**, 215–24.

Akiskal, H. S. & McKinney, W. T. (1975). Overview of recent research into depression: Integration of ten conceptual models into a comprehensive clinical frame. *Arch. Gen. Psychiat.*, **32**, 285–305.

——, Bitar, A. H., Puzantian, V. R., Rosenthal, T. L., & Walker, P. (1978). The nosological status of neurotic depression. *Arch. Gen. Psychiat.*, **35**, 756–66.

Amin, M. M. (1976). Drug treatment of insomnia in old age. *Psychopharm. Bull.*, **12**, 52–5.

Anthony, E. J. & Benedek, T. (Eds.) (1975). *Depression and human existence*. Little, Brown. Boston.

Arfwidsson, L., D'Elia, G., Laurell, B., Ottosson, J. O., Perris, C., & Persson, C. (1974). Can self ratings replace doctor's ratings in evaluating anti-depressant treatment? *Acta Psychiatrica Scandinavica*, **50**, 16–22.

Ax, A. F. (1975). Emotional learning deficit in schizophrenia. In: *Experimental approaches to psychopathology* eds. Kietzman, M. L., Sutton, S., & Zubin, J. pp. 255–68. Academic Press, New York.

Bebbington, P. (1985). Three cognitive theories of depression. *Psychol. Med.*, **15**, 759–69.

Beck, A. T. (1963). Thinking and depression. 1. Idiosyncratic content and cognitive distortions. *Arch. Gen. Psychiat.*, **9**, 324–33.

—— (1967). *Depression: Clinical, experimental and theoretical aspects.* Harper & Row, New York.

—— (1970). Cognitive therapy: nature and relation to behaviour therapy. *Beh. Ther.*, **1**, 184–200.

—— (1971). Cognition, affect and psychopathology. *Arch. Gen. Psychiat.*, **24**, 495–500.

—— (1974). The development of depression; a cognitive model. In *The psychology of depression: contemporary theory and research* (eds. Friedman, R. J. & Katz, M. M.), pp. 3–27. Winston/Wiley, Washington, D. C.

—— (1976). *Cognitive therapy and the emotional disorders*. International Universities Press, New York.

——, Feshbach, S. & Legg, D. (1962). The clinical utility of the digit symbol test. *J. Consult. Psychol.,* **26**, 263–8.

——, Kovacs, M. & Weissman, A. (1975). Hopelessness and suicidal behaviour: an overview. *J. Am. Med. Ass.,* **234**, 1146–9.

——, Laude, R. & Bohnert, M. (1974). Ideational components of anxiety neurosis. *Arch. Gen. Psychiat.,* **31**, 319–25.

——, Rush, A. J., Shaw, B. F. & Emery, G. (1979). *Cognitive theory of depression*. The Guildford Press, New York.

——, Hollon, S. D., Young, J. E., Bedrosian, R. C., & Budenz, D. (1985). Treatment of depression with cognitive therapy and amitriptyline. *Arch. Gen. Psychiat.,* **42**, 142–8.

——, Ward, C. H., Mendelson, M., Mocks, J., & Erbaugh, J. (1961). An inventory for measuring depression. *Arch. Gen. Psychiat.,* **4**, 561–71.

Becker, J. (1974). *Depression: theory and research*. V. H. Winston & Sons, Inc., Washington, D.C.

Bibring, E. (1953). The mechanism of depression. In *Affective disorders: psychoanalytic contributions to their study* (ed. Greenacre, P.). International Universities Press, New York.

Blackburn, I. M. (1975). Mental and psychomotor speed in depression and mania. *Brit. J. Psychiat.,* **126**, 329–35.

—— & Bishop, S. (1983). Changes in cognition with pharmacotherapy and cognitive therapy. *Brit. J. Psychiat.,* **143**, 609–17.

—— & Bonham, K. G. (1980). Experimental effects of a cognitive therapy technique in depressed patients. *Brit. J. Soc. Child Psychol.,* **19**, 353–63.

Blaney, P. H. (1977). Contemporary theories of depression: critique and comparison. *J. Abn. Psychol.,* **86**, 203–23.

Blatt, S. J. (1966). Review of 'Neurotic Styles' by D. Shapiro. *Psychiat.* **29**, 426–7.

—— (1974). Levels of object representation in anaclitic and introjective depression. *Psychoanal. Study Child,* **29**, 107–57.

Blumenthal, M. D. (1975). Measuring depressive symptomatology in the general population. *Arch. Gen. Psychiat.,* **32**, 971–8.

Bond, A. J. & Lader, M. H. (1974). The use of analogue scales in rating subjective feelings. *Brit. J. Med. Psychol.,* **47**, 211–18.

——, —— (1975). Residual effects of flunitrazepam. *Brit. J. Clin. Pharm.,* **2**, 143–50.

Borgatta, E. F. (1961). Mood, personality and interaction. *J. Gen. Psychol.,* **64**, 105–37.

Bower, G. H. (1981). Mood and memory. *Amer. Psychol.,* **36**, 129–48.

Bowlby, J. (1980). *Attachment and loss: Vol. III: Loss: sadness and depression*. Hogarth Press, London.

Braddock, L. (1986). The dexamethasone suppression test. *Brit. J. Psychiat,* **148**, 363–74.

Brandon, N. (1973). *The psychology of self-esteem.* Bantam Books, New York.

Breslow, R., Kocsis, J., & Belkin, B. (1981). Contribution of the depressive perspective to memory function in depression. *Amer. J. Psychiat,* **138**, 227–9.

Brown, J. & Harris, T. (1978). *Social origins of depression: a study of psychiatric disorder in women.* Tavistock, London.

Bruder, G. E., Yozawitz, A., Berenhaus, I., & Sutton, S. (1980) Reaction time facilitation in affective psychotic patients. *Psychol. Med.,* **10**, 549–54.

Byrne, D. G. (1976). Choice reaction times in depressive states. *Brit. J. Soc. Clin. Psychol.,* **15**, 149–56.

——, Boyle, D., and Pritchard, D. W. (1977). Sex differences in a self-rating depression scale. *Brit. J. Soc. Clin Psychol.,* **16**, 269–73.

Callagan, J. E. (1952). The effect of electro-convulsive therapy on the test performance of hospitalised depressive patients. Doctoral Thesis, University of London, London.

Carney, M. W. P., Roth, M., & Garside, R. F. (1965). The diagnosis of depressive syndromes and the prediction of E.C.T. response. *Brit. J. Psychiat.,* **111**, 659–74.

Carver, C. S., Ganellen, R. J., & Behar-Mitrani, V. (1985). Depression and cognitive style: comparisons between measures. *J. Pers. Soc. Psychol.,* **49**, 722–8.

Cassidy, W. L., Flanagan, N. B., Spellman, M, & Cohen, M. E. (1957). Clinical observations in manic depressive disease: a quantitative study of 100 manic depressive patients and 50 medically sick controls. *J. Amer. Med. Assoc.,* **104**, 1535–46.

Cattell, R. B. (1966). The scree test for the number of factors. *Multiv. Beh. Res.,* **1**, 245–76.

—— & Scheier, I. H. (1961). *The meaning and measurement of neuroticism and anxiety.* Ronald Press, New York.

——, Schmidt, L. R., & Bjerstadt, A. (1972). Clinical diagnosis by the objective-analytic personality batteries. *J. Clin. Psychol., Monograph Supplement,* **34**, 1–78.

Cecchini, S., Petri, P., Ardito, R., Bareggi, S. R., & Torriti, A. (1978). A comparative double-blind trial of the antidepressants caraxazone and amitriptyline. *J. Int. Med. Res.,* **6**, 388–94.

Christie, M. J. & Venables, P. H. (1973). Mood changes in relation to age, EPI scores, time and day. *Brit. J. Soc. Clin. Psychol.,* **12**, 61–72.

Ciccetti, D. V. & Prusoff, B. S. (1983). Reliability of depression and associated clinical symptoms. *Arch. Gen. Psychiat.* **40**, 987–90.

Colbert, J. & Harrow,   (1968). Psychomotor retardation in depressive syndromes. *J. Nerv. Ment. Dis.*, **145**, 405–19.

Coleman, R. E. (1975). Manipulation of self-esteem as a determinant of mood of elated and depressed womwn. *J. Abn. Psychol.*, **84**, 693–700.

Cornell, D. G., Suarez R., & Berent S. (1984). Psychomotor retardation in melancholic and nonmelancholic depression: cognitive and motor components. *J. Abn. Psychol.*, **93**, 150–7.

Coryell, W., Lavori, P., Endicott, J., Keller, M., & VanEerdewegh, M. (1984). Outcome in schizoaffective, psychotic, and nonpsychotic depression. *Arch. Gen. Psychiat.*, **41**, 787–91.

——, Lowry, M., & Wasek, P. (1980). Diagnostic instability and depression. *Amer. J. Psychiat.*, **137**, 48–51.

Costello, C. G. (1978). A critical review of Seligman's laboratory experiments on learned helplessness and depression in humans. *J. Abn. Psychol.*, **87**, 21–31.

Court, J. H. (1964). Longitudinal study of psychomotor functioning in acute psychiatric patients. *Brit. J. Med. Psychol.*, **37**, 167–73.

Cronholm, B. & Ottosson, J.-O. (1960). Experimental studies of the therapeutic action of electroconvulsive therapy in endogenous depression. The role of the electrical stimulation of the seizure studied by variation of stimulus intensity and modification by lidocaine of seizure discharge. In *Experimental studies of the mode of action of electroconvulsive therapy* (ed. Ottosson, J.-O.) *Acta Psychiatrica Scandinavica*, **145**, 69–102.

—— & —— (1961). Memory functions in endogenous depression. *Arch. Gen. Psychiat.*, **5**, 193–9.

—— & —— (1963). Reliability and validity of a memory test battery. *Acta Psychiatrica Scandinavica*, **39**, 218–34.

D'Elia, G. & Raotma, H. (1978). Reliability and validity of a nurses' rating scale for depression. *Acta Psychiatrica Scandinavica*, **57**, 269–78.

Depue, R. A. & Monroe, S. M. (1978). Learned helplessness in the perspective of the depressive disorders: conceptual and definitional issues. *J. Abn. Psychol.*, **87**, 3–20.

Derogatis, L., Rickels, K., & Rock, A. (1976). The SCL-90 and the MMPI: a step in the validation of a new self-report scale. *Brit. J. Psychiat.*, **128**, 280–9.

Donovan, D. M. & O'Leary, M. R. (1976). Relationship between distortions in self-perception of depression and psychopathology. *J. Clin. Psychol.*, **32**, 16–19.

Dorzab, J., Baker, M., Winokur, G., & Cadoret, R. J. (1971). Depressive illness: clinical course. *Dis. Nerv. Syst.*, **32**, 269–74.

Downing, R. W. & Rickels, K. (1974). Mixed anxiety-depression. *Arch. Gen. Psychiat.*, **30**, 312–17.

Dyer, J. A. T. & Kreitman, N. (1984). Hopelessness, depression and suicidal intent in parasuicide. *Brit. J. Psychiat,* **144**, 127–33.

Eysenck, H. J. (1970). The classification of depressive illness. *Brit. J. Psychiat.,* **117**, 241–50.

—— & Eysenck, S. B. G. (1976). *Psychoticism as a dimension of personality.* Hodder & Stoughton, London.

Feighner, J. P., Robins, E., Guze, S. B., Woodruff, R. A., Winokur, G., & Munoz, R. (1972). Diagnostic criteria for use in psychiatric research. *Arch. Gen. Psychiat.,* **26**, 57–68.

Fisher, K. A. (1949). Changes in test performance of ambulatory depressed patients undergoing electro-shock therapy. *J. Gen. Psychol.,* **41**, 195–232.

Fleishman, E. A. (1960). Psychomotor tests in drug research. In *Drugs and behavior* (eds. Uhr, L. & Miller, J. G.). John Wiley & Sons, New York.

Fleiss, J. L., Gurland, B. J., & Cooper, J. (1971). Some contributions to the measurement of psychopathology. *Brit. J. Psychiat.,* **119**, 647–56.

Folstein, M. F. & Luria, R. E. (1973). Reliability, validity, and clinical application of the Visual Analogue Mood Scale. *Psychol. Med.,* **3**, 479–86.

Foulds, G. A. & Bedford, A. (1975). Hierarchy of classes of personal illness. *Psychol. Med.,* **5**, 181–92.

Franz, S. I. & Hamilton, G. V. (1905). The effects of exercise upon the retardation of conditions in depression. *Amer. J. Insanity.,* **62**, 239–56.

Freud, S. (1957). Mourning and melancholia. In *Standard edition of the complete works of Sigmund Freud (Vol. 14)* (ed. and trans. Strachey, J.) Hogarth Press (originally published 1917) London.

Freyd, M. (1923). The graphic rating scale. *J. Educ. Psychol.,* **14**, 83–102.

Friedman, A. S. (1964). Minimal effects of severe retardation on cognitive functioning. *J. Abn. Soc. Psychol.,* **69**, 237–43.

—— (1970). Hostility factors and clinical improvement in depressed patients. *Arch. Gen. Psychiat.,* **23**, 524–37.

—— & Katz, M. M. (Eds.) (1974). *The psychology of depression: contemporary theory and research.* Winston/Wiley, Washington.

Frith, C. D. & Lang, R. J. (1979). Learning and reminiscence as a function of target predictability in a two-dimensional tracking task. *Quart. J. Exp. Psychol.,* **31**, 103–9.

Garvey, M. J., Schaffer, C. B. & Tuason, V. B. (1984). Comparison of pharmacological treatment response between situational and non-situational depression. *Brit. J. Psychiat.,* **145**, 363–5.

Gibson, H. B. (1965). *Manual to the Gibson Spiral Maze.* University of London Press, London.

Gitlin, M. J., & Gerner, R. H. (1986). The dexamethasone suppression test and response to somatic treatment: a review. *J. Clin. Psychiat.,* **47**, 16–21.

Glass, R. M., Uhlenhuth E. H., Hartel, F. W., Matuzas, W., & Fischman, M. W. (1981). Cognitive dysfunction and imipramine in outpatient depressives. *Arch. Gen. Psychiat.,* **38**, 1048–51.

Granick, S. (1963). Comparative analysis of psychotic depressives with matched normals on some untimed verbal intelligence tests. *J. Consult. Psychol.,* **27**, 439–43.

Greden, J. F. & Carroll, B. J. (1981). Psychomotor function in affective disorders: an overview of new monitoring techniques. *Amer. J. Psychiat.,* **138**, 1441–8.

Hall, K. R. L. & Stride, E. (1954). Some factors affecting reaction times to auditory stimuli in mental patients. *J. Ment. Sci.,* **100**, 462–77.

Hamilton, M. (1960). A rating scale for depression. *J. Neurol. Neurosurg. Psychiat.,* **23**, 56–62.

Hamilton, M. (1967). Development of a rating scale for primary depressive illness. *Brit. J. Soc. Clin. Psychol.,* **6**, 278–96.

—— (ed.) (1974). *Fish's Clinical psychopathology.* John Wright & Sons, Bristol.

—— (1976). Clinical evaluation of depressions: clinical criteria and rating scales, including a Guttman scale. In *Depression: behavioral, biochemical, diagnostic and treatment concepts* (eds. Gallant, D. M. & Simpson, G. M.), pp. 155–79. Spectrum, New York.

—— (1979). Design of clinical trials and rating scale methods. In *Psychopharmacology of affective disorders* (eds. Paykel, E. S. & Coppen, A., pp. 221–34. Oxford University Press, New York.

Hart, J., Hill, H. M., Bye, C. E, Wilkinson, R. T., & Peck, A. W. (1976). The effects of low doses of amylobarbitone sodium and diazepam on human performance. *Brit. J. Clin. Pharmacol.,* **3**, 289–98.

Healy, D., Carney, P. A., O'Halloran, A. O., & Leonard, B. E. (1985). Peripheral adrenoceptors and serotonin receptors in depression. *J. Affect. Dis.,* **9**, 285–96.

Henry, G. M., Weingartner, H., & Murphy, D. L. (1973). Influence of affective states and psychoactive drugs on verbal learning and memory. *Amer. J. Psychiat.,* **130**, 966–71.

Herbert, M., Jones, M. V., & Dore, C. (1976). Factor analysis of analogue scales measuring subjective feelings before and after sleep. *Brit. J. Med. Psychol.,* **49**, 373–9.

Heshe, J., Roder, E. & Theilgaard, A. (1978). Unilateral and bilateral ECT. *Acta Psychiatrica Scandinavica,* Suppl. **275**, 1–180.

Hiroto, D. S. & Seligman, M. E. P. (1975). Generality of learned helplessness in man. *J. Pers. Soc. Psychol.,* **31**, 311–27.

Hoffman, H. & Peterson, D. (1970) Analysis of moods in personality disorders. *Psychol. Rep.* **27**, 187–90.

Huba, G. J., Lawlor, W. G., Stallone, F., & Fieve, R. R. (1976). The use of autocorrelation analysis in the longitudinal study of mood patterns in depressed patients. *Brit. J. Psychiat.,* **128**, 146–55.

Huston, P. E. & Senf, R. (1952). Psychopathology of schizophrenia and depression. I. Effect of amytal and amphetamine sulphate on level and maintenance of attention. *Amer. J. Psychiat.,* **4**, 63–71.

Ilfeld, F. W. (1976). Further validation of a psychiatric symptom index in a normal population. *Psychol. Rep.,* **39**, 1215–28.

Izard, C. E. (1971). *The face of emotion.* Appleton-Century-Crofts, New York.

—— (Ed.) (1979). *Emotions in personality and psychopathology.* Plenum Press, New York.

Johnson, D. A. W. (1981). Depression: treatment compliance in general practice. *Acta Psychiatrica Scandinavica,* **63**, 447–53.

Johnstone, E. C., Owens, C. D. G., Frith, C. D., McPherson, K., Dowie, C., Riley, G., & Gold, A. (1980). Neurotic illness and its response to anxiolytic and antidepressant treatment. *Psychol. Med.,* **10**, 321–8.

Judd, F. K., Burrows, G. D., & Norman, T. R. (1985). The biological basis of anxiety. An overview. *J. Affect. Dis.,* **9**, 271–84.

Katz, M. M. (1971). The classification of depression: normal, clinical and epidemiological aspects. In *Depression in the 70's* (ed. Fieve, R. R.). Excerpta Medica, The Hague.

Kear-Caldwell, J. J. (1973). The structure of the Wechsler Memory Scale and its relationship to brain damage. *Brit. J. Soc. Clin. Psychol.,* **12**, 384–92.

Keller, M. B., Lavori, P. W., Rice, J., Coryell, W., & Hirschfeld, R. M. A. (1986). The persistent risk of chronicity in recurrent episodes of nonbipolar major depressive disorder: a prospective follow-up. *Amer. J. Psychiat,* **143**, 24–8.

Kendell, R. E. (1968). *The classification of depressive illness.* (Maudsley Monograph No. 18). Oxford University Press, New York.

—— (1976). The classification of depressions: a review of contemporary confusion. *Brit. J. Psychiat.,* **129**, 15–28.

Kerr, T. A., Roth, M. & Schapira, K. (1974). Prediction of outcome in anxiety states and depressive illness. *Brit. J. Psychiat.,* **124**, 125–33.

Kidman, A. (1985). Neurochemical and cognitive aspects of depression. *Prog. Neurobiol.,* **24**, 187–97.

King, H. E. (1961). Some explorations in psychomotility. *Psychiatric Research Reports,* **14**, 62–86.

—— (1965). Psychomotor changes with age, psychopathology and brain damage. In *Behavior, aging and the nervous system* (eds. Welford, A. & Birren, J.). Thomas, Springfield, Illinois.

—— (1975). Psychomotor correlates of behavior disorder. In *Experimental approaches to psychopathology* (eds. Kietzman, M. L., Sutton, S. & Zubin, J.), pp. 421–50. Academic Press, New York.

Klein, D. C. & Seligman, M. E. P. (1976). Reversal of performance deficits in learned helplessness and depression. *J. Abn. Psychol.,* **85**, 11–26.

——, Fencil-Morse, E., & Seligman, M. E. P. (1976). Depression, learned helplessness and the attribution of failure. *J. Pers. Soc. Psychol.,* **33**, 508–16.

Klerman, G. L. (1977). Anxiety and depression. In *Handbook of studies on depression*, (ed. Burrows, C. D.). Elsevier/North Holland London,

—— & Gershon, E. S. (1970). Imipramine effects upon hostility in depression. *J. Nerv. Ment. Dis.,* **150**, 127–32.

Kline, N. S. (1969). *Depression: its diagnosis and treatment.* Karger, New York.

Kolakowska, T. (1975). The clinical course of primary recurrent depression in pharmacologically treated female patients. *Brit. J. Psychiat.,* **126**, 336–45.

Kovacs, M. & Beck, A. T. (1978). Maladaptive cognitive structures in depression. *Amer. J. Psychiat.,* **135**, 525–33.

——, Rush, A. J., Beck, A. T., & Hollon, S. (1981). Depressed outpatients treated with cognitive therapy or pharmacotherapy. *Arch. Gen. Psychiat.,* **38**, 33–9.

Kringlen, E. (1985). Depression research: a review with special emphasis on etiology. *Acta Psychiatrica Scandinavica* **71**, 117–30.

Lader, M. H. (1975). *The psychophysiology of mental illness.* Routledge & Kegan Paul, London.

—— (1976). Basic trail design. *Brit J. Clin. Pharm.*, **3**, Suppl., 375–9.

—— & Wing, L. (1966). *Physiological measures, sedative drugs and morbid anxiety.* (Maudsley Monographs No. 14). Oxford University Press, London.

Lang, P. J. (1977). Imagery in therapy: an information-processing analysis of fear. *Beh. Ther.*, **8**, 862–86.

Lang, R. J. & Frith, C. D. (1981). Learning and reminiscence in the pursuit rotor performance of normal and depressed subjects. *Pers. Ind. Diff.,* **2**, 207–13.

Leckman, J. F., Weissman, M. M., Merikangas, K. R., Pauls, D. L., & Prusoff, B. A. (1983). Panic disorder and major depression. *Arch. Gen. Psychiat.,* **40**, 1055–60.

Lewinsohn, P. M. (1974). A behavioral approach to depression. In *The psychology of depression: contemporary theory and research* (eds. Friedman, R. J. & Katz, M. M.), pp. 157–78. John Wiley & Sons, London.

——, Steinmetz, J. L., Larson, D. W., & Franklin, J. (1981). Depression-related cognitions: Antecedent or consequence? *J. Abn. Psychol.,* **90**, 213–19.

Lewis, A. (1934). Melancholia: a clinical survey of depressive states. *J. Ment. Sci.,* **80**, 277–378.

—— (1936). Melancholia: prognostic study and case material. *J. Ment. Sci.,* **82**, 488–558.

—— (1938). States of depression: their clinical and aetiological differentiation. *Brit. Med. J.*, **2**, 875–8.

Lipman, R. S., Chase, C., Rickels, K., Covi, L., Derogatis, L. & Uhlenhuth, E. (1969). Factors of symptom distress. *Arch. Gen. Psychiat.*, **21**, 328–38.

Little, J. C. & McPhail, N. I. (1973). Measures of depressive mood at monthly intervals. *Brit. J. Psychiat.*, **122**, 447–52.

Lloyd, G. G. & Lishman, W. A. (1975). Effect of depression on the speed of recall of pleasant and unpleasant experiences. *Psychol. Med.*, **5.**, 173–80.

Loudon, J. B., Blackburn, I. V., & Ashworth, C. M. (1977). A study of the symptomatology and course of manic illness using a new scale. *Psychol., Med.*, **7**, 723–9.

Luria, R. E. (1974). Relationship between mood and digit-symbol performance in hospitalised patients with functional psychiatric disorders. *Psychol. Med.*, **4**, 454–9.

—— (1975). The validity and reliability of the visual mood analogue scale. *J. Psychiat. Res.*, **12**, 51–7.

—— (1979). The use of the Visual Analogue Mood and Alert Scales in diagnosing hospitaised affective psychoses. *Psychol. Med.*, **9**, 155–64.

MacFadyen, H. W. (1975). The classification of depressive disorders. Part 1. *J. Clin. Psychol., Special Monograph Supplement*, **31**, 380–401.

MacKay, C. J. (1980). The measurement of mood and psychophysiological activity using self-report techniques. In *Techniques in psychophysiology* (eds. Martin, I. & Venables, P. H.), pp. 501–62. John Wiley & Sons, Chichester.

Mackay, D. (1982). Cognitive behaviour therapy. *Brit. J. Hosp. Med.*, **25**, 242–53.

McNair, D. M. & Lorr, M. (1964). An analysis of mood in neurotics. *J. Abn. Soc. Psychol.*, **69**, 620–7.

Mahoney, M. J. (1974) *Cognition and behavior modification*. Ballinger Publishing Company, Cambridge, Massachusetts.

Maier, S. F. & Seligman, M. E. P. (1976). Learned helplessness: theory and evidence. *J. Exp. Psychol.: Gen.*, **105**, 3–46.

Marascuilo, L. A. & Serlin, R. (1977). Interactions for dichotomous variables in repeated measures designs. *Psychol. Bull.*, **84**, 1002–7.

Marks, I. & Lader, M. H. (1973). Anxiety states: a review. *J. Nerv. Ment. Dis.*, **156**, 3–16.

Martin, I. & Rees, W. L. (1966). Reaction time and somatic reactivity in depressed patients. *J. Psychosom. Res.*, **9**, 375–82.

Matussek, P., & Feil, W. B. (1983). Personality attributes of depressive patients. *Arch. Gen. Psychiat.*, **40**, 783–90.

Mayo, P. R. (1966). Speed and accuracy of depressives on a spiral maze test. *Percep. Mot. Skills.*, **23**, 1034.

—— (1967). Some psychological changes associated with improvement in depression. *Brit. J. Clin. Soc. Psychol.*, **6**, 63–8.

Meddis, R. (1969). The analysis of mood ratings. Unpublished Ph.D. Dissertation. University of London, London.

Mendels, J. (1970). *Concepts of depression*. John Wiley, New York.

—— & Cochrane, C. (1968). The nosology of depression: the endogenous reactive concept. *Amer. J. Psychiat.*, **124**, 1–11.

Miller, W. R. (1975). Psychological deficit in depression. *Psychol. Med.*, **82**, 238–60.

—— & Seligman, M. E. P. (1973). Depression and the perception of reinforcement. *J. Abn. Psychol.*, **82**, 62–73.

—— & —— (1975). Depression and learned helplessness in man. *J. Abn. Psychol.*, **84**, 228–38.

Moller, S. E., Odum K., Kirk, L., Bjerre, M., Fog-Moller, F., & Knudsen, A. (1985). Plasma tyrosine/neutral amino acid ratio correlated with clinical response to nortriptyline in endogenously depressed patients. *J. Affect. Dis.*, **9**, 223–9.

——, de Beurs, P., Timmerman, L., Tan, B. K., Leijnse-Ybema, H. J., Cohen Stuart, M. H., & Hopfner Petersen, H. E. (1986). Plasma tryptophan and tyrosine ratios to competing amino acids in relation to antidepressant response to citalopram and maprotiline. *Psychopharmacol.*, **88**, 96–100.

Morris, J. B. & Beck, A. T. (1974). The efficacy of antidepressant drugs: a review of research (1958 to 1972). *Arch. Gen. Psychiat.*, **30**, 667–74.

Morris, N. E. (1975). A group of self-instruction methods for the treatment of depressed outpatients (Doctoral dissertation, University of Toronto, 1975). National Library of Canada, Canadian Thesis Division, No. 35372.

Morrison, J. R. & Flanagan, T. A. (1978). Diagnostic errors in psychiatry. *Compr. Psychiat.*, **19**, 109–17.

Mosher, D. L. (1979) The meaning and measurement of guilt. In *Emotions and personality in psychopathology* (ed. Izard, C. E.), pp. 105–29. Plenum Press, London.

Mowbray, R. M. (1972a). The classification of depression. In *Depressive illness* (eds. Davies, B., Carroll, B. J. & Mowbray, R. M.) C. C. Thomas, Springfield, Illinois.

—— (1972b). The Hamilton Rating Scale for Depression: a factor analysis. *Psychol. Med.*, **2**, 272–80.

Mullaney, J. A. (1984). The relationship between anxiety and depression. *J. Affect. Dis.*, **7**, 139–48.

Muller-Oerlinghausen, B., Bauer, H. Girke, W., Kanowski, S., & Goncalves, N. (1977). Impairment of vigilance and performance under lithium-treatment. *Pharmakopsychiatrie*, **10**, 67–78.

Munro, A. (1966). Some familial and social factors in depressive illness. *Brit. J. Psychiat.*, **112**, 429–41.

Murphy, E. (1983). The prognosis of depression in old age. *Brit. J. Psychiat.*, **142**, 111–19.

Murphy, G. E., Simons, A. D., Wetzel, R. D., & Lustman, P. J. (1984). Cognitive therapy and pharmacotherapy, singly and together in the treatment of depression. *Arch. Gen. Psychiat.*, **41**, 33–41.

——, Woodruff, R. A., Herjanic, M., & Super, G. (1974). Variability of the clinical course of primary affective disorder. *Arch. Gen. Psychiat.*, **30**, 757–61.

Nelson, J. C. & Charney, D. S. (1980). Primary affective disorder criteria and the endogenous-reactive distinction. *Arch. Gen. Psychiat.*, **37**, 787–93.

—— & —— (1981). The symptoms of major depressive illness. *Amer. J. Psychiat.*, **138**, 1–5.

——, Jatlow, P. I., & Quinlan, D. M. (1984a). Subjective complaints during desipramine treatment. *Arch. Gen. Psychiat.*, **41**, 55–9.

——, Mazure, C., Quinlan, D. M., & Jatlow, P. I. (1984b). Drug-responsive symptoms in melancholia. *Arch. Gen. Psychiat.*, **41**, 663–8.

Ni Bhlorchain, M., Brown, G. W., & Harris, T. O. (1979). Psychotic and neurotic depression: 2. clinical characteristics. *Brit. J. Psychiat.*, **134**, 94–107.

Nie, N. H., Hull, C. H., Jenkins, J. G., Steinbrenner, K., & Bent, D. G. (1975). *Statistical package for the social sciences (SPSS)*. McGraw-Hill, New York.

Nowlis, V. (1961). Methods for studying mood changes produced by drugs. *Rev. Psychol. Appliquée*, **11**, 373–86.

—— (1970). Moods: behaviour and experience. In *Feeling and emotion: the Loyola Symposium* (ed. Arnold, M. B.). Academic Press, New York.

O'Leary, M. R., Donovan, D., Hague, W. H., & O'Leary, D. E. (1976). Distortion in the perception of depression as a function of level of depression and denial. *J. Clin. Psychol.*, **32**, 527–32.

Parker, G., Holmes. S., & Manicavasagar, V. (1986). Depression in general practice attenders; 'caseness', natural history and predictors of outcome. *J. Affect. Dis.*, **10**, 27–35.

——, Tennant, C., & Blignault, I. (1985). Predicting improvement in patients with non-endogenous depression. *Brit. J. Psychiat*, **146**, 132–9.

Pascall, G. R. & Svenson, C. (1952). Learning in mentally ill patients under conditions of unusual motivation. *J. Pers.*, **21**, 240–9.

Paykel, E. S. (1971). Classification of depressed patients: a cluster analysis of derived groupings. *Brit. J. Psychiat.*, **118**, 275–88.

—— & Weissman, M. M. (1973). Social adjustment and depression. *Arch. Gen. Psychiat.*, **28**, 659–63.

——, Prusoff, B. A., Klerman, G. L., & DiMascio, A. (1973a). Clinical response to amitriptyline among depressed women. *J. Nerv. Ment. Dis.,* **156**, 149–65.

——, Prusoff, B. A., Klerman, G. L., & DiMascio, A. (1973b). Self-report and interview ratings in depression. *J. Nerv. Ment. Dis.,* **156**, 166–82.

Payne, C. (1980). Motivational deficit in depression: people's expectations × outcome impacts. *J. Clin. Psychol.,* **36**, 647–52.

Payne, R. W. (1973). Cognitive abnormalities. In *Handbook of Abnormal Psychology* (2nd ed.) (ed. Eysenck, H. J.) Knapp, San Diego.

—— & Hewlett, J. H. C. (1960). Though disorder in psychotic patients. In *Handbook of abnormal psychology* (3rd ed.) (ed. Eysenck, H. J.). Knapp, San Diego.

Perris, C. (1973). A new approach to the classification of affective disorders. In *Aspects of depression* (ed. Garcia, R.). World Psychiatric Association, Barcelona, Spain.

——, Eisenman, M., Eriksson, U., Jacobsen, L., Knorring, L. V., & Perris, H. (1979). Variations in self-assessment of personality characteristics in depressed patients with special reference to aspects of depression. *Psychiatrica Clinica*, **12**, 209–15.

Peselow, E. D., Goldring, N., Barouche, F., & Fieve, R. R. (1985). Dexamethasone suppression test in predicting response to tricyclic antidepressants in depressed outpatients. *Psychopathology*, **18**, 206–11.

Pilowsky, I. & Spalding, D. (1972). A method for measuring depression: validity studies on a depression questionnaire. *Brit. J. Psychiat.,* **121**, 411–16.

—— & Spence, N. D. (1975). Hostility and depressive illness. *Arch. Gen. Psychiat.,* **32**, 1154–9.

Plutchik, R. & Kellerman, H. (Eds.) (1980). *Emotion: theory, research and experience,* Vol. 1. Academic Press, New York.

Post, F. (1966). Somatic and psychic factors in the treatment of elderly psychiatric patients. *J. Psychosom. Res.,* **10**, 13–19.

Preskorn, S. H. (1986). Tricyclic antidepressant plasma level monitoring: an improvement over the dose-response approach. *J. Clin. Psychiat,* **47**, 24–30.

Pribram, K. H. & McGuinness, D. (1975). Arousal, activation and effort in the control of attention. *Psychol. Rev.,* **82**, 116–49.

Prien, R. F. & Kupfer, D. J. (1986). Continuation drug therapy for major depressive episodes: how long should it be maintained? *Amer. J. Psychiat,* **143**, 18–23.

Prigatano, G. P. (1978). Wechsler Memory Scale: a selective review of the literature. *J. Clin. Psychol., Special Monograph Supplement,* **34**, 816–32.

Prusoff, B. & Klerman, G. L. (1974). Differentiating depressed from anxious neurotic outpatients. *Arch. Gen. Psychiat.,* **30**, 302–9.

——, ——, & Paykel, E. S. (1972). Concordance between clinical assessment and patient's self-report in depression. *Arch. Gen. Psychiat.,* **26**, 546–52.

——, Weissman, M. M., Tanner, J. & Lieb, J. (1976). Symptom reduction in depressed outpatients treated with amitriptyline or maprotiline: repeated measurement analysis. *Compr. Psychiat,* **17**, 749–54.

Quitkin, F. M. (1985). The importance of dosage in prescribing antidepressants. *Brit. J. Psychiat,* **147**, 593–7.

——, Rabkin, J. G., Ross, D., & McGrath, P. J. (1984a). Duration of antidepressant drug treatment. *Arch. Gen. Psychiat,* **41**, 238–45.

——, ——, ——, & Stewart, J. W. (1984b). Identification of true drug response to antidepressants. *Arch. Gen. Psychiat,* **41**, 782–6.

Rachman, S. J. (1978). *Fear and courage.* W. H. Freeman, San Francisco.

—— (1981). The primacy of affect: some theoretical implications. *Beh. Res. Ther.,* **19**, 279–55.

Rapp, W. (1978). Comparative trial of amitriptyline-N-oxide and amitriptyline in the treatment of out-patients with depressive syndromes. *Acta Psychiatrica Scandinavica* **58**, 245–55.

Raps, C. S., Reinhard, K. E. & Seligman, M. E. P. (1980). Reversal of cognitive and affective deficits associated with depression and learned helplessness by mood elevation in patients. *J. Abn. Psychol.,* **89**, 342–9.

Raskin, A. & Crook, F. H. (1976) Sensitivity of rating scales completed by psychiatrists, nurses and patients to antidepressant drug effects. *J. Psychiat.,* **13**, 31–41.

Reitan, R. M. (1955). An investigation of the validity of Halstead's measures of biological intelligence. *Arch. Neurol. Psychiat.,* **73**, 28–35.

Resnick, R. J. (1965). Hospitalization and simple reaction time. *Percep. Mot. Skills.,* **20**, 175–80.

Riskind, J. H. & Rholes, W. S. (1985). The cognitive model of depression and mood-induction procedures: a reply to Clark (1983). *Behav. Res. Ther.,* **23**, 663–6.

Rizley, R. (1978). Depression and distortion in the attribution of causality. *J. Abn. Psychol.,* **87**, 32–48.

Robertson, G. & Taylor, P. J. (1985). Some cognitive correlates of affective disorders. *Psychol. Med.,* **15**, 297–309.

Robins, E. & Guze, S. B. (1972). Classification of affective disorders: The primary-secondary, the endogenous, and the neurotic-psychotic concepts. In *Recent advances in the psychobiology of depressive illness,* (eds. Williams, T. A., Katz, M. M. & Shield, J. A.), pp. 283–93. USGPO, DPEW Publication No. (HMS) 70–9053, Washington.

——, Munoz, R. A., Martin, S., & Gentry, K. A. (1972). Primary and secondary affective disorders. In *Disorders of mood* (eds. Zubin, J, & Freyhan, F. A.), pp. 33–49. Johns Hopkins Press, Baltimore, MD.

Rochlin, G. (1965) *Griefs and discontents: the forces of change*. Little, Brown, Boston.

Roth, M. (1976). The psychiatric disorders of later life. *Psychiat. Annals*, **6**, 417–45.

——, Gurney, C., Garside, R. F. & Kerr, T. A. (1972). Studies in the classification of affective disorders: the relationship between anxiety states and depressive illnesses — I. *Brit. J. Psychiat.*, **121**, 147–61.

Rush, A. J., Beck, A. T., Kovacs, M., Weissenburger, J., & Hollon, S. (1982). Comparison of the effects of cognitive therapy and pharmacotherapy on hopelessness and self-concept. *Amer. J. Psychiat.*, **139**, 862–6.

Salzman, C. & Shader, R. I. (1979). Clinical evaluation of depression in the elderly. In *Psychiatric symptoms and cognitive loss in the elderly* (eds. Raskin, A., & Jarvik, L. F.) pp. 39–72. John Wiley & Sons, New York.

Schmale, A. H. & Engel, G. L. (1975). Conservation-withdrawal in depressive reactions. In *Depression and human existence* (eds. Anthony, E. J. & Benedek, T.) Little, Brown, Boston.

Schmickley, V. G. (1976). The effects of cognitive-behaviour modification upon depressed outpatients. Unpublished Doctoral dissertation, Michigan State University.

Schuyler, D. (1974). *The depressive spectrum*. Jason Aronson, Inc., New York.

Schwab, J. J., Clemmons, R. S., Bialow, M., Duggan, V., & Davis, B. (1965). A study of the somatic symptomatology of depression in medical patients. *Psychosom.*, **6**, 273–7.

Seitz, F. C. (1970). Five psychological measures of neurotic depression: a correlational study. *J. Clin. Psychol.*, **26**, 504–5.

Seligman, M. E. P. (1974). Depression and learned helplessness. In *The psychology of depression: contemporary theory and research* (eds. Friedman, R. J. & Katz, M. M.), pp. 83–113. Winston-Wiley, Washington, D.C.

—— (1975). *Helplessness: on depression, development and death*. Freeman, San Francisco.

—— (1978). Comment and integration. *J. Abnorm. Psychol.*, **87**, 165–179.

——, Klein, D. C., & Miller, W. R. (1976). Depression. In *Handbook of behavior modification and behavior therapy* (ed. Leitenberg, H.) Prentice-Hall, Englewood Cliffs, N. J.

Sells, S. (ed.) (1968). *The definition and measurement of mental health*. U.S. Department of Health, Education and Welfare, National Center of Health Statistics, Washington, D.C.

Shackleton, V. J. (1974). Factors affecting the declaration and communication of symptoms by psychiatric patients. *Brit. J. Soc. Clin. Psychol.*, **13**, 405–12.

Shader, R. I., Goodman, M., & Gever, J. (1982). Panic disorders: current perspectives. *J. Clin. Psychopharmacol.*, **2**, 2S–10S.

Shakow, D. & Huston, P. E. (1936). Studies of motor function in schizophrenia: I. Speed of tapping. *J. Gen. Psychol.*, **15**, 63–103.

Shapiro, M. B. (1979). The relation of guilt and other feelings to the diagnosis of depression. *Brit. J. Med. Psychol.*, **52**, 123–32.

—— & Nelson, E. H. (1955). An investigation of the nature of cognitive impairment in cooperative psychiatric patients. *Brit. J. Med. Psychol.*, **28**, 239–56.

——, Nelson, E. H. & Maxwell, A. (1960). Speed and quality of psychomotor performance in psychiatric patients. *Brit. J. Med. Psychol.*, **16**, 266–71.

——, Campbell, D., Harris, A., & Dewsbery, J. P. (1958). Effects of E.C.T. upon psychomotor speed and the distraction effect in depressed psychiatric patients. *J. Ment. Sci.*, **104**, 681–95.

Shaw, B. F. (1977). Comparison of cognitive therapy and behavior therapy in the treatment of depression. *J. Consult. Clin. Psychol.*, **45**, 543–51.

Shawcross, C. R. & Tyrer, P. (1985). Influence of personality on response to monoamine oxidase inhibitors and tricyclic antidepressants. *J. Psychiat. Res.*, **19**, 557–62.

Silberman, E. K., Weingartner, H., & Post, R. M. (1983). Thinking disorder in depression. *Arch. Gen. Psychiat*, **40**, 775–80.

Silverman, C. (1968) *The epidemiology of depression.* John Hopkins University Press, Baltimore, MD.

Simpson, G. M., Lee, J. H., Cuculic, Z., & Kellner, R. (1976). Two doses of imipramine in hospitalized endogenous and neurotic depressives. *Arch. Gen. Psychiat.*, **33**, 1093–102.

Sjöberg, L. & Johnson, T. (1976). Trying to give up smoking: a study of volitional breakdown. *Göteborg Psychol. Rep.*, **6**, no. 13.

—— & Svensson, E. (1976). The polarity and dimensionality of mood. *Göteborg Psychol. Rep.* **12**, 1–23.

Slavney, P. R., Breitner, J. C. S., & Rabins, P. V. (1977). Variability of mood and hysterical traits in normal women. *J. Psychiat. Res.*, **13**, 155–60.

Snaith, R. P., Ahmed, S. N., Mehta, S., & Hamilton, M. (1971). Assessment of the severity of primary depressive illness. *Psychol. Med.*, **1**, 143–9.

Spielberger, C. D. (1972). *Anxiety: current trends in theory and research. Vol. II.* Academic Press, London.

Spitz, R. A. (1954). Hospitalism: an enquiry into the genesis of psychiatric conditions in early childhood. *Psychoanal. Study Child*, **1**, 53.

Spitzer, R. L. & Fleiss, J. L. (1974). A re-analysis of the reliability of psychiatric diagnosis. *Brit. J. Psychiat.,* **125**, 341–7.

——, Endicott, J. & Robins, E. (1978). Research diagnostic criteria: rationale and reliability. *Arch. Gen. Psychiat.,* **36**, 773–82.

——, ——, Woodruff, R. A., & Andreason, M. (1977). Classification of mood disorder. In *Depression: Clinical, biological and psychological perspectives* (ed. Usdin, G.), pp. 73–103. Brunner/Mazel, New York.

Stallone, F., Huba, G. J., Lawlor, W. G., & Fieve, R. R. (1973). Longitudinal studies of diurnal variations in depression: a sample of 643 patient days. *Brit. J. Psychiat.,* **123**, 311–18.

Sternberg, D. E. & Jarvik, M. E. (1976). Memory functions in depression. *Arch. Gen. Psychiat.,* **33**, 219–24.

Stewart, J. W., Quitkin, F. M., Liebowtiz, M. R., McGrath, P. J., Harrison, W. M., & Klein, D. F. (1983). Efficacy of desipramine in depressed outpatients. *Arch. Gen. Psychiat.,* **40**, 202–7.

Strongman, K. T. (1973). *The psychology of emotion.* John Wiley & Sons, New York.

Sudilovsky, A., Gershon, S., & Beer, B. (eds) (1975). *Predictability in psychopharmacology: preclinical and clinical correlations.* Raven Press, New York.

Takahashi, R., Sakuma, A., Hara, T., Kazamatsuri, H., Mori, A., Saito, Y., Murasaki, M., Oguchi, T., Sakurai, Y., Yuzuriha, T., Takemura, M., Kurokawa, H., & Kurita, H. (1979). Comparison of efficacy of amoxapine and imipramine in a multi-clinic double-blind study using the WHO Schedule for a standard assessment of patients with depressive disorders. *J. Int. Med. Res.,* **7**, 7–18.

Taub, J. M. & Berger, R. J. (1974). Diurnal variations in mood as assessed by self-report and verbal content analysis. *J. Psychiat. Res.,* **10**, 83–8.

Taylor, F. G. & Marshall, W. L. (1977). Experimental analysis of a cognitive-behavioral therapy for depression. *Cog. Ther. Res.,* **1**, 59–72.

Teasdale, J. D. & Fogarty, S. J. (1979). Differential effects of induced mood on retrieval of pleasant and unpleasant events from episodic memory. *J. Abn. Psychol.,* **88**, 248–57.

——, Fogarty, S. J. & Williams, J. M. G. (1980). Speech rate as a measure of short-term variation in depression. *Brit. J. Soc. Clin. Psychol.,* **19**, 271–8.

Telner, J. I. & Singhal, R. L. (1984). The learned helplessness model of depression. *J. Psychiat. Res.,* **18**, 207–15.

Thayer, R. E. (1967). Measurement of activation through self-report. *Psychol. Rep.,* **20**, 663–78.

—— (1970). Activation states as assessed by verbal report and four psychophysiological variables. *Psychophysiol.,* **7**, 86–94.

—— (1971). Personality and discrepancies between verbal reports and physiological measures of private emotional experience. *J. Pers.*, **131**, 587–91.

Toone, B. K. & Ron, M. (1977). A study of predictive factors in depressive disorders of poor outcome. *Brit. J. Psychiat.*, **131**, 589–91.

Tsutsui, S., Yamazaki, Y., Namba, T., & Tsushima, M. (1979). Combined therapy of T3 and antidepressants in depression. *J. Int. Med. Res.*, **7**, 138–46.

Tulving, E. & Donaldson, W. (Eds.) (1972). *Organization of memory.* Academic Press, New York.

Tyrer, P. M. (1976). *The role of bodily feelings in anxiety.* Institute of Psychiatry Maudsley Monograph No. 23. Oxford University Press, London.

Uhr, L. (1960) Objectively measured behavioral effects of psychiatric drugs. In *Drugs and behavior* (eds. Uhr, L. & Miller, J. G.), pp. 610–33. John Wiley & Sons, New York.

Vaisanen, E., Naarala, M., Kontianen, H., Nerilainen, V., Heikkila, L., & Malinen, L. (1978). Maprotiline and doxepin in the treatment of depression. A double-blind multicentre comparison. *Acta Psychiatrica Scandinavica*, **57**, 193–201.

Velten, E. A. (1968). A laboratory task for induction of mood states. *Beh. Res. Ther.*, **6**, 474–82.

Walker, P. (1959). The prognosis for affective illness with overt anxiety. *J. Neurol., Neurosurg. Psychiat.*, **22**, 338–41.

Watts, C. A. H. (1966). *Depressive disorders in the community.* John Wright, Bristol.

Watts, F. N., & Sharrock, R. (1985). Description and measurement of concentration problems in depressed patients. *Psychol. Med.*, **15**, 317–26.

Wechsler, D. (1945). *Manual for the Wechsler Adult Intelligence Scale.* The Psychology Corporation, New York.

—— (1958). *The measurement and appraisal of adult intelligence.* Williams & Wilkins, Baltimore.

Weckowicz, T. E. (1973). A multidimensional theory of depression. In *Multivariate analysis and psychological theory* (ed. Royce, J. R.). Academic Press, New York.

——, Nutter, R. W., Cruise, D. G., & Yonge, K. A. (1972). Speed in test performance in relation to depressive illness and age. *Can. Psychiat. Assoc. J.*, **17**, 241–50.

——, Tam, C. I., Mason, J., & Bay, K. S. (1978). Speed in test performance in depressed patients. *J. Abn. Psychol.*, **87**, 578–82.

Weissman, M. M. & Paykel, E. S. (1974). *The depressed woman.* The University of Chicago Press, Chicago.

——, Prusoff, B., & Pincus, C. (1975). Symptom patterns in depressed patients and depressed normals. *J. Nerv. Ment. Dis.*, **160**, 15–23.

Wetzel, R. D., Margulies, T., Davis, R., & Karam, E. (1980). Hopelessness, depression and suicidal intent. *J. Clin. Psychiat*, **41**, 159–60.

White, P. B., Davis, H. K., & Cantrell, W. A. (1977). Psychodynamics of depression: implications for treatment. In *Depression: clinical, biological and psychological perspectives* (ed. Usdin, G.), pp. 308–38. Brunner/Mazel, New York.

Whitehead, A. (1974). Factors in th learning deficit of elderly depressives. *Brit. J. Soc. Clin. Psychol.*, **13**, 201–8.

Williams, H. V., Lipman, R. S., Rickels, K., Covi, L., Uhlenhuth, E. H., & Mattson, N. B. (1968). Replication of symptom distress factors in anxious neurotic outpatients. *Multiv. Beh. Res.*, **3**, 199–201.

Willner, P. (1984). Cognitive functioning in depression: a review of theory and research. *Psychol. Med.*, **14**, 807–23.

Withers, E. & Hinton, J. (1971). Three forms of the clinical tests of the sensorium and their reliability. *Brit. J. Psychiat.*, **119**, 1–8.

Woodworth, R. S. & Schlosberg, H. (1961). *Experimental psychology*. Methuen, London.

Young, J. P. R., Hughes, W. C., & Lader, M. H. (1976). A controlled comparison of flupenthixol and amitriptyline in depressed inpatients. *Brit. Med. J.*, **1**, 1116–18.

Zajonc, R. B. (1980). Feeling and thinking—preferences need no inferences. *Amer. Psychol.*, **35**, 151–75.

Zealley, A. K. & Aitken, R. C. B. (1969). Measurement of mood. *Proc. Roy. Soc. Med.*, **62**, 459–82.

Zubin, J. (1975). Problem of attention in schizophrenia. In *Experimental approaches to psychopathology* (eds. Kietzman, M. L., Sutton, S. & Zubin, J. Academic Press, London.

Zuckerman, M. (1976). General and situation-specific traits and states: new approaches to the assessment of anxiety and other constructs. In *Emotions and anxiety* (eds. Zuckerman, M. & Spielberger, C. D.), pp. 133–74. Lawrence Erlbaum Associates, New York.

Zung, W. W. K. (1965). A self-rating depression scale. *Arch. Gen. Psychiat.*, **12**, 63–70.

——, Rogers, J, & Krugman, A. (1968). Effects of electroconvulsive therapy on memory in depressive disorders. *Rec. Adv. Biol. Psychiat.*, **10**, 160–79.

INDEX